THE CUSTOMER'S
ALWAYS WRONG

THE CUSTOMER'S ALWAYS WRONG

Stupid Things Shoppers Say

GEOFF TIBBALLS

Michael O'Mara Books Limited

First published in Great Britain in 2013 by
Michael O'Mara Books Limited
9 Lion Yard
Tremadoc Road
London SW4 7NQ

A CIP catalogue record for this book is available from the British Library.

Papers used by Michael O'Mara Books Limited are natural, recyclable products
made from wood grown in sustainable forests. The manufacturing processes
conform to the environmental regulations of the country of origin.

ISBN: 978-1-78243-152-7 in hardback print format
ISBN: 978-1-78243-203-6 in paperback print format
ISBN: 978-1-78243-165-7 in e-book format

1 3 5 7 9 10 8 6 4 2

Designed and typeset by Design 23

Printed and bound by CPI Group (UK) Ltd, Croydon, CR0 4YY

www.mombooks.com

CONTENTS

INTRODUCTION

Few things are guaranteed to make our blood boil more than poor customer service. You know the sort of thing – call centres that put you on hold for forty-five minutes while forcing you to listen to an endless loop of a bored voice telling you how important your call is to them; shoe shops where the one sales assistant is too busy texting her friends about her new hair extensions to bother serving you; and so-called helplines, where the trained staff inform you that the faulty part for the new top-of-the-range, state-of-the-art, hi-tech gadget you bought for Christmas should be in around the end of February.

But maybe we should put ourselves in their shoes now and again, and consider how irritating it must be to deal with the public on a regular basis. Why should we expect bookshop staff to know the title of a particular book, based solely on the information that there is a picture of a woman on the cover and that our friend read it on holiday in 2006? How can we expect computer support staff to solve our technology problems if we persist in connecting the main hard drive cable into the back of the coffee maker? And why should travel agents tolerate us when our geographical knowledge is so abysmal that we think Bucharest and Budapest are the same place, and that the Gaza Strip is one block south of the Sunset Strip?

Packed with true anecdotes and more exchanges than you see at Marks & Spencer on 27 December, this book finally allows service staff to exact revenge on the people who make their lives a daily misery – customers.

TRAVEL TRAVAILS

AIRLINE

Flight attendant: 'Can I help you?'

Customer: 'Yes, I'm trying to sleep but there's a really loud humming noise coming from outside. Can you hear it?'

Flight attendant: 'Of course I can, sir. We all can. It's the engines.'

Customer: 'Well, can you ask the pilot to tone them down a bit? I really need to sleep before we land and I go to my meeting.'

Flight attendant: 'You want me to ask the pilot if he can turn the engines down so you can sleep?'

Customer: 'Yes please.'

Flight attendant: 'Well, you'll be sleeping for a really long time if he does what you're asking, but I'll be sure to pass the message on.'

Customer: 'Thank you.'

•

Flight attendant Monica had been enjoying an uneventful night flight until a passenger started frantically pressing his call button. When she went to investigate, he told her in a highly agitated manner that another plane was heading right for them, and urged her to tell the pilots right away. As everyone around naturally started to become concerned, Monica peered through his window but couldn't see anything untoward. He kept pointing and saying: 'There! Don't you see it? It's right there! Are you blind?' When she finally focused on the object, she immediately recognized that the 'airplane' that was about to wipe them all out was nothing more than a star. While the passenger was left suitably red-faced, Monica needed all her training and powers of self-control to be able to walk back to the galley without bursting out laughing.

•

Flight attendant: 'Is everything okay, madam?'
Customer: 'It's awfully stuffy in here. Could you open the window?'

Flight attendant: 'Would you like anything from the trolley, sir?'
Customer: 'Is there a McDonald's on board?'

•

After a busy flight had been cancelled, a lone agent was rebooking a long line of inconvenienced travellers. Suddenly an angry passenger pushed his way to the desk. He slapped his ticket down on the counter and announced:'I have to be on this flight and it has to be first class.'

The agent replied,'I'm sorry, sir. I'll be happy to try to help you, but I've got to help these folks first, and I'm sure we'll be able to work something out.'

The passenger was unimpressed. He asked loudly, so that the passengers behind him could hear: 'Do you have any idea who I am?'

Without hesitating, the gate agent smiled and grabbed her public address microphone. 'May I have your attention, please?' she began, her voice bellowing through the terminal. 'We have a passenger here at the gate WHO DOES NOT KNOW WHO HE IS. If anyone can help him find his identity, please come to the gate.'

With the people behind him in line laughing hysterically, the man glared at the agent, gritted his teeth and swore: 'F*** you.' Without flinching, she smiled and said, 'I'm sorry, sir, but you'll have to stand in line for that, too.'

•

A woman phoned an airport in a panic because she was worried that she was going to miss her flight. Breathlessly she said to the reservations clerk: 'My flight to Florida is leaving in about twenty minutes. Could you run outside and ask the pilot to wait for me?'

•

Customer: 'Why is our flight delayed? We've been sitting here for over an hour.'

Flight attendant: 'There is a mechanical problem with the aircraft, madam.'

Customer: 'Can't they just fix it in the air?'

•

A little old lady listened intently to the safety briefing before take-off. Towards the end of the talk, as the flight attendant told the passengers where to find the life jackets, the old lady raised her hand politely and said, 'I know how to swim, but where do you keep the parachutes? I don't know how to fly.'

•

With the passengers boarding the plane, flight attendant Kelly was making sure everyone remembered to store their larger items of hand luggage in the overhead lockers. As she supervised this operation, a young woman in a window seat caught her eye.

'Excuse me,' said the young woman, 'but this is my first flight and I was wondering why that hose is connected to the wing of the plane?' Kelly explained that the fuel was being pumped in and was stored in the wings. 'Oh,' replied the young woman after digesting the information. 'I guess that's why planes crash when the wings come off.'

Customer: 'What is this you've served me?'
Flight attendant: 'It's smoked duck breast, sir.'
Customer: 'Take it away. I told you I was allergic to seafood.'

•

A passenger boarded an airplane and immediately began looking under his seat. When the flight attendant asked if she could help, the passenger replied, 'Yes, I flew with your airline last year and I think I may have left my iPod on board.'

•

Customer: 'Does the airplane generate its own electricity?'
Flight attendant: 'No, sir, we just run a really, really long extension cord out behind us.'
Customer: 'Oh.'

•

Flight attendant: 'What's wrong, sir?'
Customer: 'I was hoping to see the Grand Canyon, but these clouds are in the way. Could you ask the pilot to fly a bit lower?'

HOTEL

Michael was on night duty at the front desk of a city hotel. It was four o'clock in the morning and the reception area had been quiet for two hours, allowing him to catch up with his paperwork before his shift ended at six-thirty. Suddenly, the silence was broken by the familiar 'ding' of the lift. Michael prepared himself for the inevitable interruption, but he was not ready for what appeared before him. On the other side of the front desk was a middle-aged man, standing stark naked, affording Michael a perfectly full frontal view. Fortunately, the guest did not appear particularly pleased to see him.

Behaving as if standing naked in a hotel reception in the middle of the night was an everyday occurrence, the guest calmly asked for a new room key because he had locked himself out. He gave his name, but the procedure for supplying a duplicate room key required some kind of identification. However, it did not take long to conclude that the guest was not carrying any form of ID – unless one counted the mole on his upper right thigh – so Michael decided to take his word for it. He then offered the guest his jacket to conceal his embarrassment in case they should bump into any sleepwalkers en route to the room, but the guest politely declined.

So it was that the two men came to stand side by side in the elevator – one fully clothed, the other fully exposed. For the first time Michael realized just how long the elevator took to

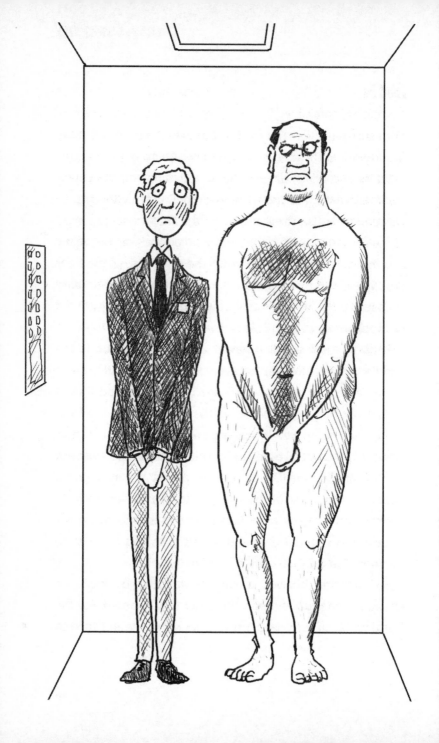

reach the fourth floor. He tried to break the awkward silence by making small talk. The weather is always a safe topic of conversation – or so he thought until he heard himself say, 'It doesn't look very nice out,' and realized that in the circumstances his remark could be badly misconstrued. Fearing that a double entendre lurked at every utterance, he remained silent for the remainder of the ascent.

Finally, the guest's naked rear end disappeared into the room. He never explained how he came to be out in the corridor in the nude at 4 a.m., and Michael was not brave enough to ask. He could only imagine that, fumbling in the dark following a toilet trip, the guest had gone through the wrong door and found himself out in the corridor, trapped and fully compromised.

•

Customer: 'Can you give me directions to Tower Bridge, please?'

Receptionist: 'Certainly, sir. Here's a map of London that shows you how to get there.'

Customer: 'Thank you. And can you tell me which side of the river Tower Bridge is on?'

•

Checking into a hotel in New Orleans, an English family announced excitedly that they had to be up early in the morning because they were off to Disneyland the next day.

Receptionist: 'That's quite a drive. What time are you hoping to get there?'

Customer: 'We thought if we left at about seven, foregoing breakfast, we should get there for eleven or twelve o'clock at the latest.'

Receptionist: 'I think you might want to take another look at your itinerary, sir. California is over 1,800 miles away!'

Customer: 'You're kidding! It looks quite near on the map – just a few inches. I can drive that distance in England in no time.'

Receptionist: 'Sir, were you be any chance basing your travel time on a world atlas?'

Customer: 'Yes. Why?'

Receptionist: 'Well, I think you'll find the map scale in a world atlas varies considerably from page to page and country to country.'

Customer: 'Oh, right. I hadn't thought of that. 1,800 miles, you say? Maybe we ought to leave at half-six, kids.'

•

Customer (on phone): 'I can't get my burrito out of the microwave in my room.'

Receptionist: 'You don't have a microwave in your room, sir.'

Customer: 'What are you talking about? Of course there's a microwave. Come and see for yourself.'

The receptionist goes up to the complainant's room.

Customer: 'There! Look! The door is shut fast. There's no way I am able to open it. Now what do you have to say?'

Receptionist: 'What I have to say, sir, is that the reason you can't get your burrito out is because you haven't put it in a microwave – you've put it in the room safe.'

•

Customer: 'Do you have any rooms for the last weekend in July?'

Receptionist: 'No, I'm sorry, we're fully booked for that weekend.'

Customer: 'Do you know if there are going to be any cancellations?'

•

A demanding guest staying at a hotel on the Canary Islands rang reception to complain that the sea was too loud. He said the noise of the waves crashing onto the nearby beach was

keeping him awake at night, and he asked the hotel staff if they could stop it. The manager replied that, whilst it was beyond his powers to control the forces of nature, he could arrange for the guest to be transferred to a quieter room on the other side of the hotel.

●

A receptionist at a Spanish hotel had just come on duty in the morning when a recently arrived English tourist came down to complain that the air conditioning in his room was so noisy that he and his wife had been kept awake all night. Saying that this was certainly not what he expected from four-star accommodation, the guest demanded to be moved to another room. The receptionist explained that the air conditioning system had only been serviced the previous week and was found to be in excellent working order. However, the guest was adamant that not only did he want a different room but he wanted to be upgraded to a superior one to compensate for the inconvenience of losing a precious night's sleep. With only one similar-quality room available for immediate occupation, before agreeing to the move the receptionist decided to call the engineer to look into the problem. Entering the English guests' room, the engineer immediately heard a low, whirring sound.

'There!' said the husband. 'I told you: noisy air conditioning.'

'I agree that it's noisy,' said the engineer, 'but it's not the air conditioning. That is located on the wall by the balcony – this noise is coming from the wall by the wardrobe.'

The engineer then opened the wardrobe door and quickly found the source of the offending noise – the guest's own electric toothbrush in his suitcase.

Following mumbled apologies supported by a claim that it was a mistake anyone could have made, the hotel staff did not receive another word of complaint from the English couple for the remainder of their two-week stay.

●

Customer (on phone): 'Hello. Is your hotel pet friendly?'

Receptionist: 'Yes, madam, we are actually one of the few pet friendly hotels in the area.'

Customer: 'Great. So what kind of pets am I allowed to have?'

Receptionist: 'Well, I guess any pet that isn't going to destroy our room.'

Customer: 'What about a goat?'

Receptionist: 'Uuuh, well I guess that would be okay as long as it didn't poop in the room or eat our cushions.'

Customer: 'It is a well-behaved and trained goat.'

Receptionist: 'Shouldn't be too much of a problem then.'

Customer: 'Great, and what about a pet fee?'

Receptionist: 'Thirty dollars, but for a goat it may be a bit more expensive just to ensure that the goat will not cause any damage.'

Customer: 'Okay.'

Receptionist: 'Anything else I can help you with today?'

Customer: 'What about seven goats?'

Customer: 'I hate these **modern** hotels with their silly room cards. Why don't you still have good old-fashioned keys?'

Concierge: 'Is there a problem, madam?'

Customer: 'Too right there is. I can't get back into my room. The card worked this morning, but now it doesn't.'

Concierge: 'Would you like me to come with you, madam, and we can try it together?'

Customer: 'Yes.'

They go to her room.

Customer: 'There. You see. I insert the card and no green light; nothing.'

Concierge: 'I can see what the problem is.'

Customer: 'So there is a fault with the card! I knew it!'

Concierge: 'No, madam, the problem is you're inserting your library card and not your room card.'

Customer: 'What?! Well, that's because my reading glasses are in my room. If I had a proper key instead of a silly card, I would have been able to fetch them.'

Concierge: 'Yes, madam.'

•

Customer: 'Is it possible for you to lower the water level in the toilet bowl in my room?'

Receptionist: 'Why, sir, is there a problem?'

Customer: 'Yes. When I sit down on the toilet, my testicles hang in the water.'

•

Customer: 'What time is the next sunset?'

Receptionist: 'Tomorrow at around 8.30.'

Customer: 'No, I mean today. What time is the next one?'

Receptionist: 'The sun already went down today – about an hour and a half ago.'

Customer: 'Yes, I know. I missed the sunset earlier. Isn't there another one soon?'

Receptionist: 'The sunset only happens once a day, ma'am.'

Customer: 'Oh.'

•

Customer: 'What time does the ten o'clock bus leave for town in the morning?'

Receptionist: 'Er, ten o'clock.'

Customer: 'Thank you.'

•

TRAVEL AGENT

Tom, a booking agent at a travel agency, was taking a reservation for a Caribbean cruise. The lady caller reeled off a long list of requirements, culminating in a demand for a basket of fruit to be placed in her room upon her arrival. However, she stated that on no account did she want grapes to be included because she considered them to be dirty and full of germs. She announced grandly: 'I only want fruit with skins I can peel off.' Furthermore, she warned that if she did find any skinless fruit, she would immediately throw the entire basket into the ocean. Tom calmly replied that as the window in her room didn't open, he would therefore have to upgrade her to a superior stateroom at a cost of $2,100. 'Is that okay?' he asked. There was a long pause before, realizing that her bluff had been called, she snapped: 'No grapes, okay?' And then she hung up.

•

Customer (on phone): 'Can you help me?'
Agent: 'I'll try, madam.'
Customer: 'I just bought a rail ticket online, and it says "Print At Home", but I need to print it now.'
Agent: 'Do you have access to a computer and printer?'

Customer: 'Yes.'

Agent: 'So what's the problem?'

Customer: 'Well, I'm not at home; I'm at work.'

•

Customer: 'I want to complain about the holiday we booked with you in Corfu.'

Agent: 'And what was the problem, madam?'

Customer: 'No one told us there would be fish in the sea. The children were scared.'

Customer: 'I'd like to complain about the holiday we booked through you in Madeira. It was nothing like it said it would be in your brochure.'

Agent: 'In what way, sir?'

Customer: 'Well, the picture of the resort in your brochure had clear blue sky, but when we were there it rained nearly every day.'

•

A lady phoned a travel agent in January wanting to know what the precise weather was going to be in Rome in the third week of June.

•

Customer: 'I want to go from Miami to Giraffe, New York.'

Agent: 'Giraffe? Are you sure that's the name of the town?'

Customer: 'Yes. What flights do you have?'

Agent: 'I'm sorry, ma'am, but I've looked up every airport code in the country and can't find a Giraffe anywhere.'

Customer: 'Oh, don't be silly. Everyone knows where it is! Check your map.'

Agent (with a flash of inspiration): 'Er, you don't mean Buffalo, do you?'

Customer: 'That's it! I knew it was a big animal!'

•

An English tourist was booking his first-ever holiday to the United States. He told the travel agent that he was particularly looking forward to visiting the Niagara Falls because he had heard so much about them, and therefore wanted to book a couple of nights at a hotel in that area. While the agent was checking online for suitable hotels, the tourist asked him: 'By the way, do you know what time they turn off the falls each day?'

•

Customer: 'I want to complain about the two-week Florida package holiday I bought from you, based in Orlando.'

Agent: 'What was wrong with it?'

Customer: 'I was expecting a hotel room with a view of the ocean.'

Agent: 'That would not be possible, sir, since Orlando is in the middle of the state.'

Customer: 'Don't lie to me. I looked on the map and Florida is a very thin state.'

•

Customer: 'I think you should warn holidaymakers that there are some unscrupulous characters along the beach area. They are just waiting to rip you off.'

Agent: 'What makes you say that, madam?'

Customer: 'Well, we bought a pair of Ray-Ban sunglasses for five euros from a street trader, and they turned out to be fake!'

•

An elderly lady called a travel agent to inquire how it was possible that her flight from Detroit left at 9.40 a.m. and arrived in Chicago at 9.53 a.m. The clerk tried to explain that Michigan was an hour ahead of Illinois, but she simply couldn't understand the concept of time zones. Finally he told her that the plane went very, very fast. The woman replied, 'Ah, that makes perfect sense.'

•

Customer: 'I wish to complain about the accommodation at the Golden Beach Hotel in the Dominican Republic.'

Agent: 'What was the problem with it, madam?'

Customer: My fiancé and I booked a twin-bedded room but instead we were put in a room with a double bed. So we hold you responsible for the fact that I now find myself pregnant. This would not have happened if we had been put in the room that we booked.'

●

Customer: 'I want to complain about your brochure for Playa del Ingles in Spain.'

Agent: 'What's wrong with it?'

Customer: 'It should be explained that the local store does not sell proper biscuits like custard creams or ginger nuts.'

●

A woman phoned a travel agent wanting to know whether airlines put physical descriptions on passengers' bags so that they could identify to whom each item of luggage belongs. The customer services adviser said he had never heard of any airline doing that and asked the woman what made her think they would. She explained that when she checked in, they put a tag on her luggage that said FAT. 'I am a little overweight,' she added. 'So I wondered if there was any connection.' The clerk said he was putting her on hold for a minute (in truth he was roaring with laughter to his colleagues) and then he came back and explained to the caller that the city code for Fresno is FAT, and that the airline was simply putting a destination tag on her luggage. It was, he assured her, nothing personal.

•

Customer: 'We're interested in visiting Lapland.'
Agent: 'Certainly, sir. I'll see what we have available. What dates were you thinking of?'
Customer: 'I'm not sure. Is Lapland open every day?'

Customer: 'I demand a full refund for our week's camping holiday at Honeysuckle Farm.'

Agent: 'Why? Was there a problem?'

Customer: 'Too right there was. Our holiday was ruined by the intrusive noise of cows mooing.'

Agent: 'But you specifically asked for a farm location, sir.'

Customer: 'I know I did. But you didn't warn me that cows moo all the time.'

●

Customer: 'I'm interested in booking two rooms for seven days at the San Lorenzo Hotel in Magaluf for some time in July.'

Agent: 'Certainly, I'll see what's available.'

Customer: 'Before you do that, there's just one thing troubling me about the hotel. In your brochure it says "No hairdressers at the accommodation", but we're all trainee hairdressers, so will it be okay for us to stay there?'

●

TAXI COMPANY

Booking clerk: 'Hello.'

Customer (on phone): 'I'd like a taxi.'

Booking clerk: 'Where do you need the cab?'

Customer: 'At my home.'

Booking clerk: 'Where is your home?'

Customer: 'I'm not giving out my address to a complete stranger. You might come and burgle my house while I'm in the taxi.'

She hangs up.

•

Ray worked as a taxi driver for more than forty years. One of his most memorable passengers was a young woman who was being taken home after what seemed to have been a long lunch. When the cab stopped at a pedestrian traffic light, she heard the beeping through the open window and asked Ray why the light always makes that noise. Ray explained that it signals to blind people when the light is red. The young woman replied in horrified tones, 'What on earth are blind people doing driving?'

•

Customer (on phone): 'I'd like to order a medium thin crust with extra cheese and tomato and a mushroom and pepperoni topping.'

Booking clerk: 'Sorry, sir, this is a cab company, not a pizza store.'

Customer: 'Are you sure?'

Booking clerk: 'Yes, sir. The last time I checked we definitely weren't baking pizzas. I can get a cab to take you to the airport or wherever you might want to go in the northern hemisphere, but if you want a margherita I'm afraid you're out of luck. This is 920 6815, the cab company. I think you want 920 6315, the pizza store.'

Customer (pause): 'So you don't do pizzas at all?'

AUTO REPAIR SHOP

A woman brought her car into an auto repair shop and told the mechanic that the vehicle kept making a strange clanking noise.

'Is there anything that brings on the noise?' asked the mechanic.

'Yes, when I drive it,' replied the customer helpfully.

After attempting in vain to identify the possible cause, the mechanic suggested taking the car for a drive. He returned thirty minutes later none the wiser, saying that the car had behaved perfectly.

He said to the customer, 'How about you drive and I'll ride with you, and as soon as you hear the noise that is troubling you, let me know.'

For the next half hour they drove around town but still the car made no unusual noises. By now the mechanic was starting to think his precious time was being wasted. Eventually the customer said: 'Oh, that's my house over there. Do you mind if I pop in to collect my grocery list?'

The mechanic wearily agreed. As the customer pulled into her drive, there was a clanking noise.

'That's it!' she yelled triumphantly. 'That's the clanking noise I've been telling you about.'

'Okay,' said the mechanic. 'Put the car into reverse.'

CLANG!

'There it is again!' said the customer.

And now forward,' said the mechanic.

CLANG!

'And again!' shouted the customer.

'Okay, stop the car,' sighed the mechanic.

He then got out, pointed to the storm drain cover on the woman's driveway and said: 'That, madam, is the cause of your clanking sound.'

●

Customer: 'I've just locked my keys in my car. Can you help me?'

Mechanic: 'Where is your car, sir?'

Customer: 'Just across the road.'

Mechanic: 'Okay, no problem. I'll pop it open for five dollars.'

Customer: 'Thanks … What are you going to do with those tools?'

Mechanic: 'I'm going to use them to open your car. I can't do it with my bare hands.'

Customer: 'Whoa! It's a brand new Mercedes. I only bought it fifteen minutes ago from the dealer. You can't touch it!'

Mechanic: 'Then how do I open it?'

Customer: 'I don't know. That's your problem.'

Mechanic: 'Actually it's your problem. I didn't lock the keys in the car.'

Customer: 'You have to open it.'

Mechanic: 'Watch me not open it.'

Customer: 'Okay then, but I'm warning you: any mark or scratch and you will have to pay Mercedes to repaint the whole car. It will cost thousands.'

Mechanic: 'So let me get this straight. If I succeed, I get five dollars. If I make the smallest mistake, it will cost me thousands of dollars?'

Customer: 'Yes.'

Mechanic: 'Your car might just be there forever.'

Customer: 'I need you to help me. I can't unlock my car. I think my key remote must be dead. It's my only car, and I'm supposed to be picking up the kids from school in half an hour. Please can you come out straight away? I don't care if you have to smash the driver's side window to get in – I must have my car on the road again.'

Mechanic: 'Okay, madam, we might not need to take such drastic action. Before we come out to you, have you tried opening the door manually by putting the key into the lock on the door?'

Customer: 'What? You can't do that with cars anymore, can you? Surely not. I bet you can't with mine.'

Mechanic: 'Give it a try, madam.'

Customer: 'Okay … Oh my God! You're right! It worked. You're my hero – you've saved my day. I never knew keys worked like that.'

•

One evening after work, a young woman called into a garage to collect her car following its annual service. Dave the mechanic was just completing the paperwork when the whole street was suddenly plunged into darkness by a power cut.

'Oh, no!' wailed the young woman. 'I won't be able to start my car.'

'Don't worry, it will start fine,' said Dave reassuringly.

'Maybe, but my headlights won't work,' she said, 'so I won't be able to see where I'm going!'

•

A young woman took her convertible sports car to a garage to be serviced on a hot summer day. The mechanic couldn't help noticing that because she had the roof down, she had caught the sun on her journey there. Her face, arms and the back of her neck were all quite red. He advised her that she should have worn sun cream. She thanked him for his concern but told him she didn't think she'd get sunburned because the car was moving.

Assistant: 'Can I help you?'
Customer: 'Yes, I'm looking for parts for my husband.'

Customer (on phone): 'Is that the auto repair centre?'

Assistant: 'Yes.'

Customer: 'I need a new clutch pedal pad for my Subaru. How much are they?'

Assistant: '£18.50.'

Customer: 'But your competitor down the street sells them for only £12.95.'

Assistant: 'Well, buy it from him then. I can't match that price.'

Customer: 'But he doesn't have any in stock.'

Assistant: 'Why didn't you say so? When we don't have any, they are only £12.95, but when we do have them they are £18.50. So do you want one or not?'

Customer (wearily): 'Okay. I'll come and pick it up in an hour.'

•

A man called his local UK car dealer to ask about legal requirements while travelling in Europe. If he purchased a car in France and then brought it back to England, would he have to change the steering wheel to the other side of the car?

LIFE EXPERIENCE

CALL CENTRE

Operator: 'Sorry, sir, I'm struggling with how to spell
   your name. Does it begin with P for Paul?'
Customer: 'No, it's the letter P.'
Operator: 'Yes, P for Paul or Peter.'
Customer: 'No, no, no. It's P for Prandesh.'

•

A call centre adviser had to phone a lady in Ohio to inform her that the balance on her phone account was overdue and needed to be settled promptly. He told her that if she didn't pay within seven days, her service would be disconnected. She calmly replied that she had written to President Obama about the matter and even though she had yet to receive a reply, the phone company should contact the White House to recover the debt.

•

Customer: 'I would like to check the status of an order, please.'

Operator: 'Certainly, madam. Can I take your name?'

Customer: 'Merry Christmas.'

Operator: 'Merry Christmas to you, too, madam.'

Customer: 'No, that's my name: Mary Christmas.'

A Chinese lady was put through to an operator at a company's Indian call centre. On realizing that she was talking to an Indian person, the woman became very excited and said how she had seen India and what a wonderful place it was. The operator asked which part of India she had visited, but the woman replied, 'Oh no, I haven't been to India. I have just seen it from the Great Wall of China.'

Customer: 'Can I put a job ad in today's paper?'

Operator: 'Sorry, the paper has already been printed and distributed. How about tomorrow?'

Customer: 'Are you sure you can't get it in today's paper? Can't you just squeeze it in somewhere? It's really important that it goes in today because we want to interview tomorrow.'

Operator: 'Sorry, it's already been printed. People have read it. What do you expect us to do – reprint the entire edition, then contact every single person who has already seen a copy and give them a replacement, just in case they want to read your ad?'

Customer: 'Yes, that would be good. And presumably I'd get a discount because the ad wouldn't be in for a full day?'

Operator: 'Dream on …'

•

Operator: 'Can I speak to the head of the household?'

Customer: 'He is busy right now.'

Operator: 'Can he come to the phone?'

Customer: 'No, he is washing his bum in front of the fire.'

Operator: 'Sorry?'

Customer: 'He is washing his bum in front of the fire and can't come to the phone.'

Operator: 'Sorry, I don't understand.'

Customer: 'You want to speak to the head of the household – that's the cat and he is washing his bum in front of the fire.'

Operator (pause): 'Maybe I'll call back.'

A man was paying by credit card over the phone after ordering a birthday gift for his daughter.

Operator: 'Okay, sir. Now I need the billing address of the card.'

Customer: 'But I want it shipped to my daughter's home.'

Operator: 'That's not a problem. I can ship it anywhere you like, but I do need the correct billing address.'

Customer: 'Okay.'

There was a long pause.

Operator: 'Sir, the billing address please?'

Customer: 'Oh, you were waiting for me? Sorry. I send the payments to a PO Box in Illinois, I think. Do you really need that address?'

Operator: 'No, sir, not where you send the payments, but where you receive the statements.'

Customer: 'A statement? Right, here's one. It says PO Box 3416, Bloomington, Illinois.'

Operator: 'Sir, is that Bloomington address you just gave me where you send your payments or where you receive your statements?'

Customer: 'Oh, the statements come here.'

Operator: 'And what is that address?'

Customer: 'But I want it shipped to …'

Operator: '… Your daughter's home. Yes, I know that, but I still need a valid billing address.'

Customer: 'Young lady, if you would just tell me what you need from me, I would be happy to supply it.'

Operator: 'Where do your credit card statements come?'

Customer: 'I told you. They come from Bloomington, Illinois.'

Operator: 'Not where they come *from*, where you receive them.'

Customer: 'In the mail, of course! You're not very smart, are you?'

Operator: 'Sir, when you receive your statement from the credit card company and open it up to look at it, where are you standing?'

Customer: 'In my kitchen.'

Operator: 'Your kitchen at home?'

Customer: 'Of course!'

Operator: 'Great! And what is your home address?'

Customer: '629, West Street, Jacksonville, Florida. If you just wanted my home address, why on earth didn't you just ask for it?'

•

Mike worked at a call centre for an electricity company. A woman once called to ask if he could turn off the power to her house because she was now at work and realized she had left her hair-curling iron on.

DIRECTORY ENQUIRIES

Caller: 'I'd like the number for a reverend in Cardiff, please.'

Operator: 'Do you have his name?'

Caller: 'No, but he has a dog called Ben.'

Caller: 'I'm looking for a knitwear company in Woven.'

Operator: 'Woven? Are you sure? I've never heard of a place with that name.'

Caller: 'Well, that's what it says on the label: Woven in Scotland.'

•

Caller: 'I'd like the number for the local RSPCA please.'

Operator: 'Where are you calling from?'

Caller: 'The living room.'

•

Caller: 'The Water Board please.'

Operator: 'Which department?'

Caller: 'Tap water.'

•

Caller: 'I need a phone number for a guy in Munich.'

Operator: 'Okay, the code for Germany is …'

Caller: 'He's not in Germany, he's in Munich.'

•

Caller: 'I'd like the number of the Argoed Fish Bar in Cardiff, please.'

Operator: 'I'm sorry, there's no listing. Are you sure the spelling is correct?'

Caller: 'Well, it used to be called the Bargoed Fish Bar but the B fell off.'

•

A female operator was alarmed to receive a call from a man accompanied by the sound of heavy breathing. First he gave the name of the company he wanted, followed by heavy breathing, then he gave the address, again followed by heavy breathing. Finally she told him that she was going to hang up unless he cut out the heavy breathing. 'Oh no,' he said. 'It's not what you think. You see, I'm in a phone box but I haven't got a pen, so I'm steaming up the window to write the number on!'

HOME IMPROVEMENT STORE

Customer: 'I need some nails. Can you help me?'

Assistant: 'Certainly, sir. How long do you want them?'

Customer: 'Oh. I was rather hoping to keep them.'

Philip was aware of a customer who had been going up and down the aisles for ten minutes or more, clearly searching for something. Although it was store policy not to hassle customers, Philip finally decided it was time to go over and ask the man if he needed any help. 'Yes,' muttered the man, still scanning the shelves, 'where do you keep the left-handed spanners?'

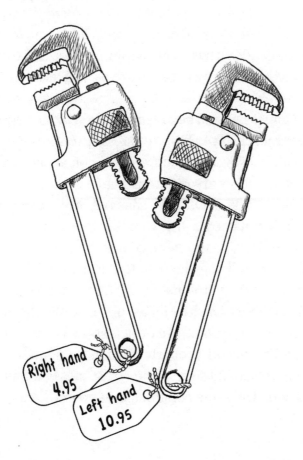

Right hand 4.95

Left hand 10.95

Lorraine worked on the paint desk at a large out-of-town DIY store. One day a man came in with a paint chip from a previous order several years ago and said he needed to touch up some scratches. Many of the paint names and numbers had recently been changed, so when the customer showed Lorraine the chip she had to look it up on the computer to achieve the right match. When she found it, she presented the result to the customer.

Customer: 'No that's the wrong colour. This one's called jade green and the one you have is teal green.'

Lorraine: 'I know. They changed the colour names a few months ago. They're the same colour.'

Customer: 'No, they're different. Look at the names. The numbers are different, too.'

Lorraine: 'I know. They changed the colour and number names a few months ago. Compare the chips. They're the same colour, see?'

Customer: 'But they have different names.'

Lorraine: 'I know the names aren't the same, sir, but the colours on the chips are exactly the same colour as the paint. We even test the paint to make sure it's mixed properly by putting some on the chip to see if it's the same. Trust me, teal green is exactly the same colour as jade green.'

Customer: 'But why would they be the same colour if they have different names?'

Lorraine: 'Because they changed the names a few months ago … ?'

Customer: 'Why would they do that?'

Lorraine: 'I don't know, sir. Perhaps they did it to make dealing with customers like you even more challenging.'

•

Customer: 'I bought these two tins of paint from you last week, but I've changed my mind about the colour scheme, so I'd like to return them.'

Assistant: 'Do you want to buy new tins or do you want your money back?'

Customer: 'I'd like my money back.'

Assistant: 'Okay. That's £20.'

Customer: 'No, it should be £40.'

Assistant: 'How come?'

Customer: 'Look at the receipt.'

Assistant: 'Yes, I can see you bought the paint under a buy one, get one free promotion, but I can only give you back what you paid, and that's £20.'

Customer: 'But the tins of paint are worth £20 each! If I can't return them for full price you're ripping me off. It's not buy one get one free if I can't return them for full price.'

Assistant: 'I'm sorry, but I can't give you more for the paint than you paid originally. If you had paid £40, I would give you back £40, but because you only paid £20, I'm only giving you £20. You're getting your money back. It seems like a simple concept to me.'

Customer: 'So the whole offer is a lie. You're nothing but a bunch of crooks. I'll be writing to someone about this.'

•

Working on the customer service desk at her store, Michelle suddenly became aware of three large trees slowly approaching her from the direction of the fitted bathrooms section. At first, she thought she must be hallucinating after an especially arduous day, but then it dawned on her that the trees were real and were on store trolleys with their price tags still attached. As the arboreal menace moved ever closer, she could see that they were being pushed by a small woman who was dwarfed by the conifers and whose face was almost completely concealed behind the foliage, as if she were on army camouflage training in the jungle. On finally reaching the desk, the woman stepped out from behind the mobile forest and announced herself to Michelle. She produced the receipt for the trees and said she wanted to return them because – an excuse Michelle had never heard used before in her fifteen years of retail – her neighbour had threatened to kill them. Seeing Michelle's instinctive double take, the woman elaborated: 'He said they were an eyesore and that I had better get rid of them or he would kill them.' There was clear panic in the woman's voice as she said this, as if these trees were people that her neighbour was going to kill in front of her like a brutal sacrifice.

'What do you mean, he's going to kill them?' spluttered Michelle.

'He's going to poison them!' hissed the woman, checking over her shoulder in a state bordering on paranoia. 'I just can't let him do that. I have to get my money back or else he'll kill them!' Sensing that the woman's fear was genuine, but suspecting that the police might not put the threat to two junipers at the top of their list of priorities in a city rife with gun crime, Michelle felt she had no option but to refund her money. Relieved, the woman then said goodbye to the trees like a single mother reluctantly giving up her children for adoption: she knew they would probably never meet again but was sure that one day they would be grateful to her for allowing them to move to a home where they could live happily – apart from the occasional squirrel incursion.

•

Customer: 'I've been calling 0800 1800 for three days but I can never get through to your enquiry desk.'

Assistant: 'Where did you get that number from, sir?'

Customer: 'It was on the entrance door of your store.'

Assistant: 'Sir, those are our opening hours.'

BANK

Customer: 'I'd like to borrow £2,000.'

Clerk: 'Certainly, sir. Over how long?'

Customer: 'Three years, please.'

Clerk (operating calculator): 'That will be £75 a month for thirty-six months. Is that okay?'

Customer: 'No, it's not. I want it all at once.'

•

Customer: 'I haven't received my quarterly bank statement.'

Clerk (checking computer): 'That's odd. We sent it to 26 Quarry Lane. Is that your address?'

Customer: 'No, I've moved.'

Clerk: 'When did you move?'

Customer: 'Six weeks ago.'

Clerk: 'And did you notify us of your new address?'

Customer: 'No, I haven't had time. Anyway, what does that matter? You should have sent it to the correct address. I've half a mind to cancel my account – you people are so incompetent.'

•

Customer: 'I've lost my password for my online account.'

Clerk: 'Did you write it down somewhere?'

Customer: 'No, because I read that you shouldn't leave it anywhere where burglars might find it.'

Clerk: 'So what did you do?'

Customer: 'I wrote it on the back of my hand. But this morning I forgot and had a shower.'

•

Clerk: 'Now for security purposes, sir, I need your mother's maiden name.'

Customer: 'Oh dear, I can't remember it. How awful! But I can remember my father's maiden name. Will that do?'

Clerk: 'You'll probably find that's the same as your own surname, sir.'

Customer: 'Yes, you're absolutely right. How did you know?'

•

Customer: 'I'm calling about the personalized security questions I had to enter to access my online bank account.'

Clerk: 'Why? Is there a problem?'

Customer: 'Well, I used the title of my favourite song, but that was two years ago and now I have a new favourite song, so do I have to change it?'

•

A clerk at the UK HQ of a global bank was on the phone giving a computer password to a colleague in another country.

Clerk: 'So your password is London1, L-O ...'

Caller: 'Hello?'

Clerk: 'Can you hear me?'

Caller: 'Yes, yes.'

Clerk: 'So I was saying that your new password is London1. It is spelt L-O ...'

Caller: 'Hello?'

Clerk: 'Do you understand what your password is?'

Caller: 'No.'

Clerk: 'Right, then I'm going to spell it out for you. Okay?'

Caller: 'Yes.'

Clerk: So you spell your password L-O ...'

Caller: 'Hello? Hello?'
Clerk: 'I'll tell you what. Your new password is Berlin1.
　　Okay? Have a good day.'

Customer (on phone): 'Is the manager there?'
Clerk: 'I'm sorry. He's on holiday.'
Customer: 'I'll hold.'

An elderly lady phoned her bank's call centre to say that she had received all of the documentation and passwords required to operate her first-ever online account. Aware that online banking does not always come naturally to some people, the clerk asked the lady whether she understood everything about the process. 'Oh yes,' the lady replied cheerfully. 'It's all perfectly clear – oh, apart from one small thing. When I make a withdrawal from my online account, how long does it usually take for my computer printer to print out the bank notes?'

Clerk: 'Thank you for calling. My name is Karen. How may I help you?'

Customer: 'Without my knowledge, my teenage daughter has used my credit card to buy concert tickets. That's $200 missing from my account. I've torn up the tickets, and I would like you to refund me the money.'

Clerk: 'I'm sorry, madam, if it was a legitimate purchase, there's nothing we can do. She bought the tickets and received them, albeit without your approval.'

Customer: 'Well, she's a spoilt, uncontrollable brat! Can anything be done about that?'

Clerk: 'I'm afraid I can't help you with that either, madam, but maybe you could try a Juvenile Correctional Facility.'

•

Customer: 'I'd like to cash this cheque.'
Clerk: 'Have you any identification on you, sir?'
Customer: 'No.'
Clerk: 'Driver's licence? Passport?'
Customer: 'No.'
Clerk: 'I'm afraid I can't cash this cheque without seeing some form of identification.'
Customer: 'I suppose you could read the messages on my mobile phone. That way you'd know it was me.'

•

Customer (on phone): 'Is that the City Bank call centre?'
Clerk: 'It is, madam, and my name is Harry. How may I help?'
Customer: 'Well, my name is Mrs. Gomersall and I phoned my branch at West Street, Newtown, with a query, but they wouldn't talk to me. They said it was company policy not to deal with customer

questions over the phone but to refer all enquiries to the bank's call centre. Is that correct?'

Clerk: 'Yes, madam. We can answer any question just as well – if not better – than your local branch.'

Customer: 'Oh, good. In that case can you tell me whether I left my gloves in there this morning?'

INSURANCE COMPANY

Customer: 'I took out an insurance policy with your company twenty-five years ago for £100,000 and I'd like to cash it in.'

Adviser: 'Can I have your name and the policy number please, madam?'

Customer: 'Yes, it's Mrs. Betty Wilkinson and the policy number is 44512.'

Adviser: 'Thank you. And can I have the first line of your address?'

Customer: '463 Main Street.'

Adviser: 'Okay … well looking at your policy details I'm afraid we can't pay out yet.'

Customer: 'Why not?'

Adviser: 'Because it's a life insurance policy.'

Customer: 'What difference does that make?'

Adviser: 'The policy is on the life of Betty Wilkinson and that's you, right?'

Customer: 'Correct.'

Adviser: 'Well, a life policy is only payable upon death, and unless I'm very much mistaken, Mrs. Wilkinson, you're not dead yet.'

Customer: 'Huh! Typical insurance company. I knew you'd start splitting hairs. Goodbye!'

Working at an insurance company call centre, Sasha took a call from a female customer who wanted a reading.

'A reading?' queried Sasha.

'Yes, a reading,' confirmed the caller. 'I usually have Elaine. Is she there?'

Sensing that the caller had her wires crossed, Sasha informed her that this was the Acme Insurance Company.

'No it's not,' said the caller. 'It's the psychic line.'

Having received several calls for tarot card readings that week, Sasha explained to the caller that she had dialled the wrong number and needed to add an extra zero for the psychic hotline. The caller was highly indignant. 'I really think you should tell people at the start,' she bristled. 'I've been on hold for half an hour.'

Sasha decided against pointing out that the caller had had to press three options and listen to a tape with frequent messages about insurance policies for thirty minutes, yet had still failed to realize that she was not about to be put through to someone with a crystal ball.

•

Customer: 'Does your European Breakdown Policy cover me when I'm driving in Australia?'

Adviser: 'I think you'll find the clue is in the name of the product, sir.'

Customer: 'Oh, yes. I hadn't thought of that.'

As part of the information required for setting up a home contents and buildings policy, the insurance company operator needed to know how many people lived in the policyholder's house.

'Just a minute,' replied the caller, and there was silence. The operator waited patiently for the caller to return but it was another ten minutes before his voice was heard again.

'Where have you been?' asked the operator.

'I was fetching a tape measure to work out the size of the house,' said the caller. 'I make it 1,800 square feet.'

•

Adviser: 'Okay, madam, to insure your car, I need to know the year it was built, the make and the model.'

Customer: 'It's a 1999 Toyota.'

Adviser: 'And what sort of Toyota is it exactly?'

Customer: 'A white one.'

•

FUNERAL PARLOUR

Undertaker: 'Do you want your wife to be buried with any of her favourite things?'

Customer: 'That's a nice idea. Do you think the cat will mind?'

Customer: 'I'd like to send a bouquet of flowers to my wife. It's her birthday tomorrow.'

Undertaker: 'Has your wife died?'

Customer: 'No, of course not!'

Undertaker: 'Well, I'm sorry, sir – not for the fact that your wife hasn't died because I'm very happy to hear that she's still alive – but this is a funeral parlour, not a florist.'

Customer: 'Then why have you got flowers in the window?'

Undertaker: 'What do you suggest we put in the window, sir?'

•

A middle-aged woman called into a funeral parlour to make arrangements for the cremation of her mother. The undertaker went through all the details and informed the woman how much it would cost. He said that out of respect for the customer's feelings at such a difficult time it was not the practice of the firm to send out a full invoice until after the service, but he did ask whether she would mind paying a small deposit in advance.

She agreed and asked if it was okay to pay by cheque. That was not a problem, he said, but he asked if she had some form of identification on her to serve as authorization.

She immediately reached into her handbag and pulled out her driving licence but he couldn't help noticing that her date of birth had been covered up with Tipp-Ex. Puzzled, but aware of the need for sensitivity, he gently asked for her date of birth and she told him it was 26 April 1955.

Needing to guarantee the cheque, he decided to type the information into the computer to make sure everything was above board, but was alarmed when the computer reported that the woman's name and address did not match her date of birth. Hesitantly he tackled her over the discrepancy and asked her whether the date she had given him was a fake. 'Of course it is,' she replied shamelessly. 'I'm an actress!'

SHOPPING SHAME

CLOTHES STORE

Customer: 'I'd like to return this sweater I bought last week. It has a hole in it. Here is the receipt.'

Assistant: 'Sorry, madam, according to the receipt you didn't buy the sweater from this store. You bought it from Topshop. You'll have to take it there.'

Customer: 'What does it matter? You have exactly the same sweater on your racks. I can see it from here. Just give me a refund.'

Assistant: 'I'm sorry, I can't do that.'

Customer: 'Why not?'

Assistant: 'Well, if you bought a packet of salad from Tesco and found a dead mouse in it, you wouldn't take it back to Sainsbury's, would you?'

Customer: 'You're talking hypothetical nonsense now. There's clearly no point in trying to have a sensible conservation with you.'

•

June was working in the menswear section of a clothing store when a Japanese tourist came in wanting to buy a pair of trousers. She showed him several pairs in his chosen style and colour until eventually he found a pair he liked. But before she had a chance to direct him to the changing room, he simply dropped his trousers in front of her, revealing a pair of tight-fitting Y-fronts, in full view of the other customers. Reacting quickly, June scooped up the old and new trousers and physically dragged the bewildered tourist – in his underpants – to the nearest changing room, praying that they would get there before her supervisor spotted them. 'There, there, you do it there,' she said, pushing him behind the curtain, 'or police come with their flashy blue light.' The poor man looked horrified and was so shaken by the experience that he couldn't bring himself to make the purchase.

Customer: 'Uh, I'd like to exchange these underpants that I bought here six months ago.'

Assistant: 'Any particular reason?'

Customer: 'Yeah. There's a mark on them.'

Assistant: 'So I can see. And was that mark there when you bought them?'

Customer: 'Uh, I'm not sure. Maybe.'

Assistant: 'I don't think so, sir. This mark is recent, and judging by its position and colour I'd say it's the result of the garment being worn, if you get my drift.'

Customer: 'Are you saying it's a skid mark?'

Assistant: 'Yes.'

Customer: 'Well, it's not mine.'

Assistant: 'Well, they're your underpants, sir. Who else is going to be wearing them?'

Customer: 'I guess my flatmate could have borrowed them without telling me.'

Assistant: 'Your flatmate is in the habit of borrowing your underpants?'

Customer: 'Sometimes. So it's not my fault. He didn't tell me. So will you exchange them?'

Assistant: 'No, sir. I suggest you ask your flatmate to get you a new pair. And after that I suggest you get a new flatmate.'

●

Customer (reading assistant's name tag): 'Jasmine. That's a pretty name.'
Assistant: 'Thank you.'
Customer: 'Where did you get it?'

•

Customer: 'I'm looking for some underwear.'
Assistant: 'Okay, sir.'
Customer: 'To be specific, I'm looking for underpants that don't chafe. I'm eighty-two, you see, and when you get to my age things get a little tender down there, so I can't be doing with pants that rub me or I'll be fidgeting all day. So which can you recommend?'
Assistant: 'I'd really like to help you, sir, but in case you hadn't noticed I'm wearing a skirt and I have breasts. In short, I'm a woman and as such I've never worn any of these brands of men's underpants nor have I any intention of starting.'
Customer: 'So you don't know which ones will be gentle on my balls?'
Assistant: 'No, sir, I'm afraid I don't. But if you wait here a minute I'll fetch my colleague Derek. He's always got his hands down his pants, so I'm sure he'll be happy to advise you.'

•

Customer: 'I wanted some denim shorts but I can't find any, so can I buy these jeans and cut off the legs when I get home?'

Assistant: 'You can do whatever you like with them once you've bought them.'

Customer: 'But can I cut the legs off?'

Assistant: 'Sure.'

Customer: 'Would I be able to return them if I make a mess of it?'

Assistant: 'With the legs cut off? Sorry, no.'

Customer: 'That's not good customer service.'

Customer: 'Do you work here?'

Assistant: 'Yes.'

Customer: 'Is this a thin tie?'

Assistant: 'Yes, that is a thin tie.'

Customer: 'How do you know?'

Assistant: 'Well, you see, it's thinner than the other ones.'

•

Assistant: 'Madam, your son is climbing that rail of expensive designer shirts. Would you please make him stop?'

Customer: 'Don't you tell him off! All boys like to climb. It's not his fault that there's nothing interesting for him to do in this shop. Anyway I hope it's not going to fall on him. It should be secure, you know.'

•

Alison's first job on leaving school was working in a city centre ladies' fashion store. One day she was confronted with the customer from hell. The customer in question was a smartly dressed, middle-aged businesswoman who wanted a refund for a skirt she had bought there. Unfortunately, she did not have the receipt for the skirt, without which Alison was unable to process the refund. When Alison explained this, the woman became hysterical and yelled: 'What do you mean? I shop in here all the time! You should know who I am!' Alison told her that if she could find the receipt, she would happily refund it, but without it there was nothing she could do. Hearing this, the woman began rummaging angrily through her bag and her handbag, scattering the contents over the store floor. Other shoppers cowered behind racks of dresses or hid in changing rooms, anxious not to make eye contact with the fearsome woman. Finally she screamed: 'I can't find the goddamned receipt! You can keep the f***ing skirt!' She then hurled the garment at Alison and stormed out.

An hour later, Alison's manager, who had been out of the store during the commotion, took a phone call in his office. It was the customer in floods of tears. 'Tell that poor girl I'm so sorry for my behaviour,' she sobbed. 'I don't know what came over me.'

The woman still visits the store from time to time, but continues to be so embarrassed by her outburst that if she sees Alison is working on the tills she browses through the racks of clothes until Alison's shift is over. Her record browsing time is said to be an hour and a half.

•

GREETING CARD SHOP

Customer: 'I want my money back because I cut my finger on the corner of one of your cards. The corners are way too sharp, so I demand a full refund. In fact, you're lucky I'm not taking you to court over the injury.'

Assistant: 'I'm sorry to hear of your misfortune, madam, but all of our cards are cut as standard at a ninety-degree angle.'

Customer: 'Well, it's not good enough. In future they should all be cut with a curved edge.'

Assistant: 'How do you cope with sheets of paper? They have sharp edges, too.'

Customer: 'That's different. Paper is that shape anyway. It's your cards I'm talking about.'

Assistant: 'Madam, paper is cut that way, just like our cards.'

Customer: 'You're trying to confuse me. I want round corners on your cards in future. Understood?'

Assistant: 'Sure, madam. We'll look into it.'

•

Customer: 'I want to buy a Kim Jong-il.'
Assistant: 'A what?'

Customer: 'A Kim Jong-il. Oh, sorry, I have trouble remembering the names of items, so I use word association. I want to buy a short ruler.'

Assistant: 'Oh, a Nicolas Sarkozy. Why didn't you say?'

•

Customer (on phone): 'Can I speak to Chris Hickson?'

Assistant: 'There is no Chris Hickson here.'

Customer: 'There must be. He works in the recycling department.'

Assistant: 'This is not recycling. We are a greeting card shop in Winchester.'

Customer: 'Well, do you know Chris's number?'

SHOE SHOP

Customer: 'You have a pair of black brogues in the window, priced £99.99. Could I try them on please?'

Assistant: 'Certainly, sir. What size?'

Customer: 'Size 11 for the right foot and size 10 for the left.'

Assistant: 'Come again …'

Customer: 'I have different sized feet. So I need a size 11 shoe for my right foot and a size 10 for my left.'

Assistant: 'I'm sorry, sir, that's two separate pairs of shoes. You'll need to have them specially made by a craftsman.'

Customer: 'Why? You have the shoes I want. Where does it say I can only buy them as a standard pair?'

Assistant: 'Look, sir, if you want odd shoes from this shop, you'll have to buy both pairs.'

Customer: 'Why should I pay double?'

Assistant: 'Because otherwise we're going to be left with a pair of shoes comprising a size 10 right foot and a size 11 left foot.'

Customer: 'Well, you might get another customer like me.'

Assistant: 'I very much doubt that, sir.'

•

Customer: 'I bought these sandals from this store last year and kept them at our beach house. But one day I forgot my water shoes, and so I had to wear these in the ocean instead. As a result the Velcro came off and now they're useless. I want to exchange them for a new pair.'

Assistant: 'Are you kidding me?! Sorry, but we have no guarantee that our leather sandals can be worn in the ocean as swimming shoes.'

Customer: 'Well, I certainly won't be shopping here again!'

•

Customer: 'I need a pair of shoes.'

Assistant: 'Okay, sir, what size do you want?'

Customer: 'I don't care, as long as it fits.'

Assistant: 'Well, is there any particular style you prefer?'

Customer: 'I don't care, as long as it fits.'

Clerk: 'I'm sorry, sir, but I cannot bring the entire stockroom out here for you to try on.'

•

Customer: 'I'm looking for a pair of white heels suitable to wear at a wedding.'

Assistant: 'No problem. We have a large range over here.'

Customer: 'But I also want to be able to go hiking and maybe even climbing in them. So they must be

sturdy, waterproof and have good arch support.'

Assistant: 'Let me get this clear: you want a pair of white climbing boots with heels?'

Customer: 'No, I don't want boots. I can't wear boots to my friend's wedding! I want a pair of elegant, feminine heels that can also cope with rocky terrain and all weathers. But I don't want pointy toes because they give me bunions. And they must be in buttersoft leather because anything rough will rub into my prominent ankle bone.'

Assistant: 'Right. Have you ever seen a pair of shoes like this?'

Customer: 'No, but that's your job to find me some, isn't it?'

•

Customer: 'I bought these shoes for my three-year-old son only ten months ago, but now they don't fit him. Can I have a refund?'

Assistant: 'On what grounds?'

Customer: 'They're the wrong size.'

Assistant: 'But they weren't the wrong size when you bought them for him, were they, madam?'

Customer: 'That's beside the point. They don't fit him now.'

Assistant: 'That's because his feet have grown. That's what children's feet do. It's if they don't grow that you need to worry. And unless you intend squeezing his feet into size three shoes until he's eighteen, I'm afraid that's something you're going to have to come to terms with.'

Customer: 'But there's nothing wrong with them apart from the size. Can't you buy them back off me and give them to homeless people?'

Assistant: 'We tend not to get too many homeless three-year-olds around here.'

Customer: 'Huh! So what do you suggest I do?'

Assistant: 'Get pregnant again?'

•

Customer: 'I've been on the internet and seen a brand of shoes that are sold only in Europe.'

Assistant: 'A brand of shoes, you say, sold only in Europe?'

Customer: 'Yes, that's right?'

Assistant: 'And do you know where you are now, madam?'

Customer: 'Washington, DC.'

Assistant: 'Correct.'

Customer: 'So do you have them?'

OPTICIAN

Receptionist: 'Thank you for calling Beechwood Opticians. How can I help you?'

Customer: 'I want to check on the status of my glasses.'

Receptionist: 'Okay. Can I have your full name please?'

Customer: 'Lindsey Robertson.'

Receptionist: 'And how do you spell your first name?'

Customer: 'L-I-N-D-S-E-Y.'

Receptionist: 'Thank you. I'll just put you on hold for a minute, madam … Okay, I can't find your name on the computer, and I've checked all other spellings of your first name. Would you mind giving me your date of birth?'

Customer: '9-8-81.'

Receptionist: 'Well, there is a Lindsey corresponding with that date of birth but … would you by chance be listed under another name?'

Customer: 'No.'

Receptionist: 'Okay, I'll try searching by address.'

Customer: '44, Virginia Avenue.'

Receptionist: 'Right, well I seem to have you listed on the computer as Lindsey Thomas.'

Customer: 'That's not me.'

Receptionist: 'Well, the date of birth matches, as does the address. Would you like me to search by social security number?'

Customer: 'That's not my name, I tell you. I got married and my last name is Robertson now.'

Receptionist: 'I'm sorry, your insurance company still has you listed as Thomas, so that's how we got mixed up. You'll need to call them to get it updated.'

Customer: 'That's no excuse.'

Receptionist: 'I'm sorry, but there was no way for us to know you got married.'

Customer: 'But it was in the newspaper!'

•

An optician remembers a young woman coming in for her first eye test. He measured the vision in both of her eyes by getting her to wear the standard metal testing frame into which he then inserted various lenses. Afterwards, he asked her what she thought. Looking at herself in the mirror, she said, 'I can see much better, but I was rather hoping for smarter frames.'

•

Customer (paying by card): 'Oh dear, I've forgotten my PIN. I know it's the day and year of my eldest daughter's birthday, but I can't remember when she was born. Do you happen to know?'

•

Optician: 'Would you like to complete our short survey and get ten per cent off?'

Customer: 'Yes. No problem.'

Optician: 'Okay. If you wouldn't mind filling out the survey on the computer and then I'll put it through.'

Customer: 'I don't understand.'

Optician: 'If you fill out the survey on the computer, I can give you the discount. All you have to do is click yes or no and then the "Next" button.'

Customer: 'It sounds terribly complicated and I don't use computers … Can I still have the ten per cent off?'

•

DEPARTMENT STORE

A young girl was serving on the perfume counter of a major department store when an imposing-looking woman walked in. The woman clearly had fake breasts, hair extensions, false eyelashes, false nails and was wearing layers of make-up that looked as if it had been applied with a trowel. She haughtily picked up a bottle from the counter, looked at the young sales assistant and demanded, 'This fragrance: is it natural?'

•

Customer: 'I bought this Nintendo Wii Fit Plus from you last month and I want to return it to you.'

Assistant: 'Okay, madam, what seems to be wrong with it?'

Customer: 'It's inaccurate, that's what's wrong with it!'

Assistant: 'In what way?'

Customer: 'It describes me as obese. Can you believe that?!'

Assistant: 'Er, well ...'

Customer: 'No way am I obese! No way!'

Assistant: 'Well, how can I put this, the Wii Fit Plus does have a good reputation for reliability.'

Customer: 'Are you calling me fat?'

Assistant: 'No, I was just saying ...'

Customer: 'You are! You're calling me fat! How dare you! Just because I'm not anorexic like you! You look as if you need a good meal. I tell you, it's not healthy for a girl to be that skinny. Size zero; you'll waste away in ten years.'

Assistant: 'Let's not get personal, madam. In any case I'm sure at worst you're just borderline ...'

Customer: 'I haven't eaten solids for two days since getting that cruel read-out. I lie awake at night fretting about my weight. I don't want to face the world because I think everyone is staring at me, saying, "Look at her, see how obese she is." Not just a pound or two overweight; obese, like a beached whale. I'm a nervous wreck thanks to this thing. It's got me down so much I'm thinking of jumping off a bridge. I just don't see the point of living anymore. So are you going to give me my money back?'

Assistant: 'In the circumstances, perhaps we can agree to a refund.'

Customer: 'Thank you. I don't really think you're anorexic. You don't think I'm obese, do you? Tell me honestly. I can take it.'

●

Customer: 'Hello, young man, I've just bought my first computer and I need some printer ink.'

Assistant: 'What make printer do you have?'

Customer: 'I've got it written down here: it's an HP Deskjet D1460.'

Assistant: 'And do you want a black or a colour ink cartridge?'

Customer: 'Oh, they do colours, do they? Wonderful! Right, I'll have purple and grey.'

Assistant: 'No, that's not quite how it works, sir. The printer has one colour cartridge and that's able to do all the colours.'

Customer: 'Really? How are they able to fit all the colours into one cartridge? I mean, there are so many colours in the world. There are all the ones in the rainbow, and then you've got things like turquoise, lilac and maroon.'

Assistant: 'They only put blue, red and yellow in the cartridge, and they're mixed to make all the colours.'

Customer: 'Even magnolia?'

Assistant: 'I'm not sure about that, sir. Magnolia's not going to show up too well on white paper.'

Customer: 'Good point. Anyway, it sounds amazing, but there's just one thing that puzzles me: how will the printer know which colour goes where if I don't tell it? I don't want to end up with red grass.'

•

A woman went into a department store to buy a small disposable barbecue. The barbecues were little metal trays full of coal wrapped in a protective box, which featured a picture of a family happily cooking. The customer bought one and took it home, but upon opening it decided it needed to be returned. The reason she gave the baffled sales assistant, upon making the return, was that the food that was in the picture on the front of the box wasn't included inside.

A lady customer stopped by the haberdashery department of a store.
Customer: 'Can you cut some cloth for me?'
Assistant: 'Certainly. What width?'
Customer (annoyed and slightly confused): 'Scissors, of course!'

•

Browsing the cosmetics counter in a department store, a woman customer brazenly took an unopened jar of face cream out of its box, unscrewed the lid and put some on her face. Before the sales assistant could say anything, the woman said, 'Yes, this is fine. I'll take it.' But as the sales assistant took the jar to wrap it, the woman barked, 'No, no, my dear, I don't want that one. It's been opened!'

PET SHOP

Customer: 'I want you to spank my son.'
Assistant: 'What?!'
Customer: 'He's been playing me up all morning, so I told him that if he didn't behave, the scary-looking man in the pet store would spank him.'

Assistant: 'Spank your own damn kid, lady!'
Customer: 'I don't believe in spanking!'
With that, she stormed out.

Customer (on phone): 'Hi, I'd like to know what kind of hamster food you guys have. I'm looking for one type, but I don't know what it's called.'

Assistant: 'Well we stock Living World, Scarlett, Kaytee, Vitakraft and about six others.'

Customer: 'I'm still not sure.'

Assistant: 'Okay. What does the food look like? What's in it?'

Customer: 'I don't know. My daughter feeds the hamster, not me.'

Assistant: 'Well, what did the package look like?'

Customer: 'I'm not sure. Wait, it had a picture of a hamster on it!'

•

Customer: 'Do you groom cats?'

Assistant: 'Yes. They need to be up-to-date with their rabies shots and you need to make an appointment.'

Customer: 'He doesn't get shots.'

Assistant: 'He needs a rabies shot to get groomed.'

Customer: 'Well, he doesn't have one. Why can't you groom him without one?'

Assistant: 'For safety reasons, it's our policy, madam. If an animal bites you …'

Customer (interrupting): 'You just don't want to groom him because he bites. That's it, isn't it?'

Assistant: 'If he does bite, he really needs that paperwork.'

Customer: 'Well, the other groomers didn't require it and they didn't need stitches either!'

She then walked out.

•

Customer: 'I'd like you to clip my little Yorkie.'

Assistant: 'Any special requests, madam?'

Customer: 'Yes, I'd like you to leave some curtains underneath so that his boy parts don't show, and also could you avoid making his rectum look like a target?'

POST OFFICE

Elderly customer: 'I'd like to buy a first-class stamp for an email.'

Clerk: 'Do you mean air mail, madam?'

Customer: 'No, I mean a letter that I send on my computer. My daughter told me it's called an email.'

Clerk: 'Yes, that's right, it is an email, madam, but you don't need a stamp for it.'

Customer: 'Not even a second-class stamp?'

Clerk: 'No, nothing. It's free. It's electronic. That's what the "e" stands for.'

Customer: 'Oh, how wonderful! I think I'm going to enjoy having a computer after all.'

•

Customer: 'I need to send a letter to my daughter in Albania, but I can never remember which country it's in.'

Clerk: 'Albania is a country.'

Customer: 'No, it's not. You're thinking of Alberta.'

Clerk: 'But that isn't a country.'

Customer: 'Of course it is! My goodness! With people like you working in the Post Office no wonder she never seems to get my letters!'

•

An elderly lady went into a Post Office in Wales and wanted to know how much it would cost to send a letter by airmail to Walsall. When the postmistress pointed out that you don't need air mail for Walsall, the old lady protested: 'Are you sure? Isn't it the capital of Poland?'

•

Customer: 'I'd like forty Christmas stamps, please – but none with holly on them. I don't mind robins, reindeer and Santa, but not holly.'
Clerk: 'What's wrong with holly?'
Customer: 'I'm allergic to holly. It brings me out in a rash. So I'm certainly not going to lick it.'

•

A customer is staring at the branch's opening hours on a stand in front of the counter.
Clerk: 'Can I help you?'
Customer: 'What is "20:00"?'
Clerk: '20:00 means p.m.'
Customer: 'Oh. You should put the times in English.'

LEISURELY PURSUITS

PUBLIC LIBRARY

Customer: 'Do you accept donations of old books?'
Librarian: 'Certainly, madam.'
Customer: 'Good. I also have a few late books. Do I return them here?'
Librarian: 'Yes … Actually, madam, you have £12 in fines on these.'
Customer: 'Um … okay … Is there any way of trading the books I'm giving to you as credit toward the fines? Or is there no chance of that happening?'
Librarian: 'There's no chance of that happening.'
Customer: 'Okay.'

•

Shona was working in a public library when a customer asked for the name of the movie in which Shakespeare starred. Shona asked the woman if she was referring to the recently released *Shakespeare in Love*. The customer replied that Shakespeare was her favourite author and she knew there was a movie that he had actually appeared in. Shona tried to explain to the woman that Shakespeare had died three-hundred years before movies were invented, but she remained defiant and left saying that she was going to try Blockbuster.

•

Librarian: 'Can I help you?'

Customer: 'Yes. Can you tell me where I get the shower tokens?'

Librarian: 'Shower tokens? This is a library.'

Customer: 'Yes, I know. But a guy I met in the street told me the showers here are free.'

Customer (on phone): 'My nine-year-old son is in your library at the moment. He has brown hair, is medium height and is wearing a black and white T-shirt, blue jeans and red trainers.'

Librarian: 'Okay, madam, is there a message you want me to pass on to him?'

Customer: 'No, just don't let him check out any books on ghosts and witches. That's all. Thank you. Goodbye.'

●

In over twenty years as a librarian, Janet had heard a variety of odd and eccentric requests, yet she was to discover she had not heard them all, when a man came up to her desk and asked, 'Do you have a life-sized globe in the library?'

Janet considered the implications of the request for a second before asking disbelievingly, 'Are you sure you mean life-sized?'

The man was adamant that he did. Not wishing to make the customer appear foolish, she quietly suggested that a large globe would surely suffice, as a life-sized one would actually be the size of Earth itself. Having pointed this fact out to him, she expected the penny to drop and for him to laugh at his gaffe, but instead he just looked at her blankly and replied, 'Yes, life-sized.' Realizing that he was unable to appreciate the ridiculousness of his demand and that he was clearly not going to back down, Janet came up with the most diplomatic response she could muster, 'Sorry, sir, the life-sized globe's in use at the moment.'

●

Customer: 'I'm searching for a book by J.D. Salinger, but I've been looking around this section for fifteen minutes and I can't find his books anywhere. Why are they all listed by numbers instead of the author's last name?'

Librarian: 'That's because you're in the non-fiction section, sir. See the sign? J.D. Salinger wrote fiction. That's on the next floor.'

Customer: 'Oh, is there a difference between fiction and non-fiction?'

●

Customer: 'Can you answer me a question?'

Librarian: 'I'll try.'

Customer: 'Can you tell me why so many famous Civil War battles were fought on National Park sites?'

●

An old man spent some time looking through the cassettes and CDs that made up the extensive audiobook collection at a public library. Eventually he went over to the librarian and said, 'Excuse me, but will the little rectangular ones play in the player meant for the round flat ones?'

•

Customer: 'I'm looking for a hardback book with about four-hundred pages.'

Librarian: 'Any particular subject?'

Customer: 'It doesn't matter what it's about; it's the size that's important.'

Librarian: 'I understand. You just want a meaty book that you can get your teeth into?'

Customer: 'No, our kitchen table is wonky. I need it to prop up one of the legs.'

•

Customer: 'I'd like to take out this book *How* to *Hug*.'

Librarian: 'I'm sorry but I can't let you take that book out of the library.'

Customer: 'Why not?'

Librarian: 'Because it's volume seven of the encyclopedia.'

•

Librarian: 'Can I help you, madam?'

Customer: 'Yes. Which power sockets in the library are appropriate for my hairdryer?'

•

Customer: 'Do you have a copy of Oscar Wilde's *The Importance of Being Earnest?*'

Librarian: 'I'll just check if it's in stock.'

Customer: 'I want to borrow it because that was my father's name.'

Librarian: 'What, Oscar?'

Customer: 'No, Ernest.'

•

Customer (in writing): 'Where are the encyclopedias?'

Librarian (slowly, so the librarian can lip read): 'One floor up – '

The customer gestures for the librarian to write, who assumes he can't lip read. The customer goes on his way after reading the instructions. Suddenly there is a loud noise, and he looks towards the sound.

Librarian: 'I thought you couldn't hear!'

Customer (in writing): 'Stop talking, this is a library!'

•

Customer: 'Do you have any books about Vlad the Impaler?'
Librarian: 'Yes, I think so.'
Customer: 'I don't want anything gruesome, though.'

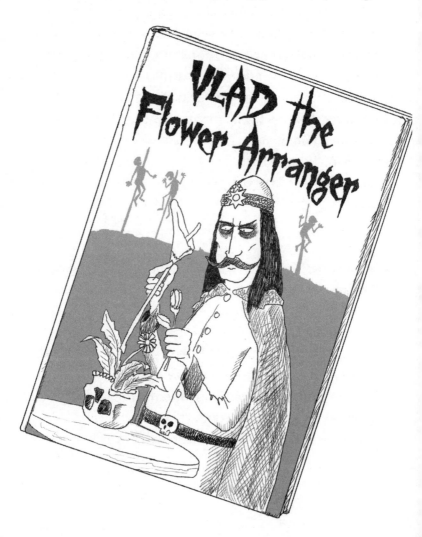

A junior librarian became aware of a minor commotion at the self-checkout machine, where a woman said she had just checked out a book but now couldn't locate it. She searched her bags, pored through piles of discarded books and looked under the library computers but couldn't find the missing tome anywhere. Meanwhile, two helpful members of staff checked the return bins and even the library washroom, which the woman had just visited, but all to no avail. In despair, the woman threw her hands in the air and wailed, 'I don't know where it can be!'

Hearing this, the junior librarian offered to help. 'What's the title of the book?' she asked.

The woman replied straight-faced: *'How To Organize Your Mind.'*

•

Customer: 'I've got a terrible rash on my neck. Let me show you.'

Librarian: 'Oh, yes, that is bad.'

Customer: 'What do you think it could be?'

Librarian: 'I'm sorry, madam, but I'm a librarian, not a doctor.'

Customer: 'But surely you must have some idea?'

Librarian: 'No, you should go and see your doctor.'

Customer: 'I hate going to see him. I always have to wait for ages. Couldn't you just look up my symptoms on your computer?'

CINEMA

Customer: 'What time is the next showing of *Ghost Rider: Spirit of Vengeance*?'

Usher: '8.45.'

Customer: 'That's another hour I've got to wait! Can't you put it on early just for me?'

Usher: 'No, I'm afraid we can't. We have our set session times. The last one was 6.30 and the next one is 8.45.'

Customer: 'Well, there's no one else here to see the movie, so I don't see why you can't.'

Usher: 'The reason there's no one else waiting out here in the foyer at the moment is because they're either inside watching the 6.30 screening or they're waiting to come for the advertised time of 8.45.'

Customer: 'Well, that's not good enough. I can't wait an hour. Surely you don't want to turn away custom? Don't you people have any initiative? I want to see the manager because you obviously don't know what you're talking about.'

The usher summons the manager.

Manager: 'What seems to be the problem?'

Customer: 'The movie I want to watch isn't on until 8.45, but I want to watch it now otherwise by the time it finishes I'll miss my last train home.'

Manager: 'Hmmm. Okay. I see your predicament, but I don't understand what you expect me to do about it. We can't just change the schedule to suit you.'

Customer: 'But like I explained to your dimwit assistant here, there's nobody else waiting.'

Manager: 'And as I'm sure he explained to you, that's because they will arrive for the advertised time.'

Customer: 'Huh, I might have known you people would stick together. Well, you won't be getting my custom again, I can promise you!'

Manager: 'I'm sure we'll cope with that loss, sir.'

•

Customer: 'Do you have any tickets left for the 7.30 screening tonight?'

Usher: 'Sorry, we're sold out, but I can fit you in tomorrow night or Monday.'

Customer: 'No, I wanted tonight. Are you sure there are no seats left?'

Usher: 'Yes, I'm afraid we're full.'

Customer: 'It's only for two people.'

Usher: 'Sorry, there's nothing left for tonight. Do you want me to book you in for tomorrow?'

Customer: 'Could you just check again for tonight? There are only two of us.'

Usher (glancing at computer screen): 'No, still sold out. What other nights can you do? The film's on here for another three weeks.'

Customer: 'Couldn't you just put an extra couple of seats in the aisle for us tonight?'

Usher: 'Seats in the aisle? No way! What would happen if there was a fire?'

Customer: 'Don't worry about us. We'd be first out.'

Usher: 'There are no seats for tonight. Goodbye.'

•

Working as an usher in a cinema, David was standing at the back of the auditorium, monitoring the matinee audience. The showing was barely half full, so he was anticipating a quiet couple of hours before the next batch of moviegoers arrived. However, halfway through the film he heard a voice call out in a loud whisper, 'Young man! Young man!' He shone his torch to locate the voice and found that it belonged to an elderly lady six rows down who was turning around and waving her arms to attract his attention. He went over to investigate and asked her what the problem was. 'Young man,' she said, 'since the theatre isn't full, would it be possible for you to pause the film while I go to the toilet?'

•

A cinema was looking to recruit new staff, so the manager attached a sign to the box office saying 'Accepting Applications'. On the first day, a man came in and asked for a ticket to see *Accepting Applications*. Although the staff explained to him that it was not the title of a movie but that they were accepting applications for employment, he still left shaking his head and muttering something about going to see it at the other cinema in town.

DVD RENTAL STORE

Elderly customer: 'Do you happen to know whether I've ever borrowed *One Flew Over the Cuckoo's Nest* before?'

Assistant: 'Can I have your name and address, sir?'

Customer: 'George Matthews, 247 Union Street.'

Assistant: 'Right, Mr. Matthews, according to our records it looks like you borrowed that movie on the eighth of December last year.'

Customer: 'Thank you, young man. Tell me, did I enjoy it?'

•

Customer: 'I took out this DVD of *Pulp Fiction* last week, and I want a refund.'

Assistant: 'Why, is there a fault on the DVD?'

Customer: 'Not as far as I can tell.'

Assistant: 'Then why do you want a refund on the movie?'

Customer: 'I didn't like it. It was too violent.'

•

Customer: 'I want to rent this DVD for tonight. Can you tell me how long it is?'

Assistant: 'It says on the box: 110 minutes.'

Customer: 'Damn! I've only got an hour to watch it. When I bring it back tomorrow, can you tell me what happens in the end?'

•

Back in the days of VHS, two elderly Italian men went into a video store to complain that the tape they had rented wasn't working. The assistant decided to play it to see what the problem was but as soon as she opened the box one of the men became really excited and said to his friend, 'Oh, Luigi, first you have to open the box and *then* put it in!'

•

Customer: 'I took out the DVD of *The Elephant Man*, and I really enjoyed it. Do you have any more movies with him in?'

Assistant: 'Er, no, madam, as far as I know the Elephant Man was only in one movie.'

Customer: 'That's a shame. He was so good in it.'

•

Customer: 'What's the scariest movie you have?'

Assistant: 'Well, it's a matter of personal taste, sir, but this one features a zombie invasion, graphic scenes of bloody mutilation, a chainsaw murder, an acid attack and a particularly explicit decapitation and disembowelment.'

Customer: 'It's not a musical is it? I hate musicals.'

●

Assistant: 'How can I help you?'

Customer: 'I have spent two days trying to rewind a DVD. How do you do it?'

●

Customer: 'I saw a film on TV back in the 1980s. It was a comedy. I can't remember the title but I think there was an American actor in it. Do you know the one I mean?'

●

Assistant: 'Okay, ma'am, these are due back on Friday before midnight.'

Customer: 'Oh. Do I have to return them?'

BOOKSHOP

Customer: 'What's this?'
Bookseller: 'A boxed set of *The Lord of the Rings*.'
Customer: 'But the third one isn't in the cinema yet.'
Bookseller: 'They're the books.'
Customer: 'They made books of it?'

•

A woman went into a bookstore and asked for help with finding a particular book. After the sales assistant had successfully located the book on the shelves, the woman said, 'Thank you. Could you get me a copy?'

The assistant looked puzzled and asked, 'What's wrong with this one?'

The woman replied haughtily: 'I don't want a display copy, dear. I want one I can take home!'

•

Customer: 'I'm looking for a book on British birds.'
Bookseller: 'Certainly, sir. We have several.'
Customer: 'But I don't want one that includes the magpie.'
Bookseller: 'But the magpie is a British bird.'

Customer: 'I know, but I don't like them. They're nasty, noisy, thieving creatures that steal other birds' eggs. And they peck my plants. So do you have any books featuring all British birds except the magpie?'

Bookseller: 'No, sir. I'm sorry, all the books on British birds that we stock will include the magpie. Of course, you could buy the book and then tear out the page with the magpie on it.'

Customer: 'What, and ruin a perfectly good book? Are you mad?'

Customer: 'I'm looking for a particular book.'

Bookseller: 'What book are you looking for?'

Customer: 'I don't know the title or the author's name.'

Bookseller: 'Is there anything at all you know about the book?'

Customer: 'I know it has a blue cover.'

Bookseller: 'We have several hundred books with blue covers. Is there anything else you can tell me to help narrow it down a little?'

Customer: 'I think it was supposed to be funny.'

Bookseller: 'Well, I could show you to our extensive humour section and you could have a look through there.'

Customer: 'You're joking! I haven't got all day. All I wanted was one book and you've completely wasted my time!'

•

Customer: 'I want to book a flight to Denver.'

Bookseller: 'This is a bookstore, madam.'

Customer: 'That's right. I want to book a flight.'

Bookseller: 'No, I'm sorry, madam. We don't do that. We sell books that people read.'

Customer: 'Well, who should I call then?'

Bookseller: 'Try an airline. I've heard they're quite good with flights.'

Customer: 'Do you have any books on advanced particle physics?'
Bookseller: 'We may have.'
Customer: ' … Suitable for a five-year-old.'

Serving in her small independent bookshop, Ellen became aware of a man behaving furtively. Twice he approached the cash desk as if to ask for assistance, only to back away when another customer entered the shop. Eventually the shop emptied and he headed straight for the desk where, leaning over conspiratorially, he whispered to Ellen, 'Do you have any books on masturbation?'

'We do have a few sex books,' she replied, desperately trying to stifle a giggle. 'Or of course you could try the self-help section.'

Not convinced that she was taking his request seriously, he marched straight out of the shop, crashing into the full-size promotional cutout of Delia Smith with such force that he ended up on the floor, legs wrapped around the cutout's midriff. Judging by the smile on Delia's face, she had enjoyed the tumble a lot more than the customer, who knelt on the floor, glowering at Ellen.

•

Customer: 'Do you have any good books?'

Bookseller: 'Well, I like to think that most of the books we sell are good, although I'm sure there are one or two duds.'

Customer: 'Right. Well, what's the best book you sell?'

Bookseller: 'Surely you appreciate that I haven't read

every book in the store ...'

Customer: 'What do you mean you haven't read every book? Why not? That's your job. How else can you recommend stuff to customers?'

Bookseller: 'Sir, we stock over 4,000 books. Much as I like reading, there aren't enough hours in the day to read every book.'

Customer: 'Listen, I want your recommendation. Tell me what your favourite book is.'

Bookseller (randomly): 'That one.'

Customer: 'Thank you. I'll buy it. But if I don't enjoy it, I'll be back.'

•

Customer: 'Have you got *Fifty Shades of Grey*?'

Bookseller: 'Certainly.'

Customer: 'Have you read it? Be honest, woman to woman, does it work?'

Bookseller: 'Let's just say I have friends who have adopted it enthusiastically.'

Customer: 'Have you tried any of the practices it mentions?'

Bookseller: 'I get enough pain and humiliation coming into work each day.'

Customer: 'Oh, right. And do you sell the accessories –

you know, handcuffs, ball gags and nipple clamps?'

Bookseller: 'I'm afraid you'll have to go to a sex shop for those.'

Customer: 'That's a shame. I'm too shy to go into one of those places. I think I'd die of embarrassment. You couldn't order me some, could you? I think my nipples are probably size large, don't you?'

•

Customer: 'Can you tell me which Maeve Binchy books I haven't read yet?'

Bookseller: 'Er, *Circle of Friends*?'

Customer: 'No, I've read that.'

Bookseller: '*Heart and Soul*?'

Customer: 'No, I've read that.'

Bookseller: '*Scarlet Feather*?'

Customer: 'Read that, too.'

Bookseller: 'Might it be easier if you told me the Maeve Binchy books that you have already read?'

Customer: 'No, I can only remember them when I hear the title.'

•

John was working in a rural Yorkshire bookshop when an American lady, who was on holiday in the area, walked in and began browsing the shelves. She asked if John could recommend something for her to take to her sister back home in Idaho. He suggested *Pride and Prejudice* by Jane Austen as it's a great favourite with women. The American lady was so thrilled with the idea that, as she paid for it, she said to John: 'We're flying home on Friday. Do you think there is any chance that Jane Austen could sign the book for me before we leave?'

Bookseller: 'Can I help you?'

Customer: 'Yes. Do you have any books with photographs of dinosaurs?'

●

Customer: 'Do you have any books on Adolf Hitler?'

Bookseller: 'Yes, we have two or three in stock, I think.'

Customer: 'Have you ever read any?'

Bookseller: 'I can't say I have, but books about him still sell well.'

Customer: 'I read one last month. It was called *The Secret Life of Adolf Hitler*, and it told me things about him that I never knew. For instance, apparently when he was having sex he liked to pee on people.'

Bookseller: 'Really?'

Customer: 'Yes. Disgusting, isn't it? It put me right off him.'

●

A lady walked into a bookstore and asked the sales assistant if he had any novels by the Russian author Anna Karenina.

●

Customer: 'Do you have a threesis?'

Bookseller: 'A what?'

Customer: 'A threesis. You must know it. It has other words that mean the same as the word you look up.'

Bookseller: 'You mean a thesaurus?'

Customer: 'Don't be stupid. That's a dinosaur. No, I want a threesis.'

Customer: 'Do you think there'll be a new Barbara Cartland book out this year?'

Bookseller: 'I don't think she'll be writing any new books, given that she died in 2000.'

Customer: 'So you don't even think it's worth me going on a waiting list, just in case?'

●

Customer: 'Can you recommend a book for me?'

Bookseller: 'What sort of things are you interested in?'

Customer: 'All kinds of subjects, but I'm a manic depressive, so I'd prefer not to have anything with a black cover.'

●

Customer: 'I've got a book here and it's so good that I'd like to order another copy for my sister.'

Bookseller: 'Certainly, sir. Can you give me the title and author, please?'

Customer: 'Yes, it's *Holidays in Cornwall* by Michael Scott.'

Bookseller: 'And can you read me the barcode?'

Customer: 'Oh, where's that?'

Bookseller: 'On the back of the book, sir.'

Customer: 'Ah, right. Yes, it's black bar, grey bar, black bar, white bar …'

•

Customer: 'You should be ashamed of yourself selling all these *Harry Potter* books.'

Bookseller: 'Why? They're very popular.'

Customer: 'Because they're full of wizards, and wizards corrupt young minds. They are the tool of the devil.'

Bookseller: 'Right. So what sort of books do you think we should be stocking?'

Customer: '*The Lord of the Rings*.'

Bookseller: 'But what about Gandalf? How is it okay for him to be a wizard?'

Customer (angrily): 'Gandalf is not a wizard! Do you hear me? He is not a wizard!'

•

An American tourist walked into a bookstore in England and said she was looking for something to improve her mind. After thinking for a moment or two about what best to recommend, the bookseller asked, 'Have you read Shakespeare?'

'No,' said the tourist. 'Who wrote it?'

Customer: 'There doesn't seem to be a price on this book. How much is it?'

Bookseller: 'That particular title is £120.'

Customer: '£120 for a book?! Are you crazy?'

Bookseller: 'It's a rare first edition from 1884. That's why it's so expensive.'

Customer: 'If it's that old it should be dirt-cheap. You should be giving it away.'

Bookseller: 'But it's an original and very collectible.'

Customer: 'Well, not by me it isn't. I wouldn't give you more than a pound for it. Look at it, the pages are all yellow and it smells kind of musty.'

Bookseller: 'You haven't really grasped the concept of antiques, have you, sir?'

•

Customer: 'Do you have any books about the impressionists?'

Bookseller: 'You mean Monet, Renoir and Degas?'

Customer: 'Yeah, possibly, but as long as it also features Rich Little.'

•

Customer: 'Excuse me, do you have an erotica section?'

Bookseller: 'Yes, sir, just over there.'

Customer: 'Thank you. Tell me, if I pay for a saucy book on my credit card you won't tell anyone, will you?'

Customer: 'Hi, I'm looking for a book I heard about on the radio.'

Bookseller: 'Okay. What's the title?'

Customer: 'I don't know.'

Bookseller: 'That's okay. Do you remember the author?'

Customer: 'No.'

Bookseller: 'Hmmm. What about the show it was on?'

Customer: 'Nope.'

Bookseller: 'Oh, well … what was it about?'

Customer: 'I don't know.'

Bookseller: 'Fiction? Non-fiction? Anything come to mind at all?'

Customer: 'No, but I really want to read it.'

Bookseller: 'Sorry, sir, but we're only psychic on Tuesdays.'

●

Customer: 'I'd like to buy that book by Agatha Christie.'

Bookseller: 'Which one?'

Customer: 'Oh, has she written more than one?'

Bookseller: 'Yes, madam, she's written a lot more than

one.'

Customer: 'In which case I don't know. I think there's a detective in it investigating a murder.'

Bookseller: 'That's not really narrowing the field down much, I'm afraid.'

Customer (exasperated): 'Very well, I'll have to go home and ask my daughter. Call yourself a bookshop!'

HAIRDRESSER

Customer (on phone): 'I'd like to book an appointment for today with Carla.'

Receptionist: 'I'm sorry, Carla's on holiday today.'

Customer: 'She can't be! I need her. I have an important conference to attend, and she always does my hair.'

Receptionist: 'I'm sorry, she had two days' leave to take, so she's taken them today and tomorrow. But she'll be back on Wednesday. I could try and book you in for then.'

Customer: 'Don't be so stupid. My conference is tomorrow!'

Receptionist: 'Well, we have other stylists, madam.'

Customer: 'I don't want other stylists! I want Carla! How could she do this to me? It's unforgivable.'

Receptionist: 'Look, madam, Janine is very experienced and has won lots of awards. She had a cancellation this morning, so she has a slot at 3.45. I'm sure she'd be happy to do your hair.'

Customer: 'Well, I suppose she'll have to do. But it's not good enough. Carla shouldn't be allowed to take a holiday.'

●

As a hairdresser, Sandy liked to experiment with her hair colour, switching from red to blue to purple as the fancy took her. On this particular day it was a vivid cerise, a colour usually seen only on a blushing flamingo. Midway through the morning she had an appointment with a new customer who immediately began admiring her hair. She gushingly told Sandy that she loved the style, the texture, but above all, the outrageous shade of pink. Finally, leaning closer, she said to Sandy, 'Your secret is safe with me, but tell me, do you colour it?'

●

Customer: 'When would be the best time to bring my two-year-old son in for a haircut?'

Receptionist: 'When he's four.'

●

Jenny was working in a New York hair salon when an Italian woman came in to buy a wig. The customer must have tried on more than forty hairpieces in different colours and styles until she finally found one that she liked. 'How much is this one?' she asked. Jenny told her that it was $340, plus tax. The woman gasped: '$340?! You're kidding me! And forget the tax; I'll use glue.'

Hairdresser: 'I'm afraid I won't be able to cut your daughter's hair today, Mrs. Jones.'

Customer: 'Why not?'

Hairdresser: 'Because it's against our policy to cut anybody's hair if they have lice.'

Customer: 'Lice? Lice? What are you talking about? She can't have lice! She goes to a private school!'

•

Customer: 'I want to complain about the haircut one of your stylists gave me yesterday.'

Hairdresser: 'What's wrong with it?'

Customer: 'He cut it too short, so I want it cut again.'

Hairdresser: 'But if he cuts it again, it's going to be even shorter.'

Customer: 'Oh yeah. I hadn't thought of that.'

EXTREME TECHNOPHOBIA

COMPUTER SUPPORT 1

Technician: 'You're through to Customer Support. You're speaking to Gary. How can I help you?'

Customer: 'I bought a new computer from your damn store this morning and it's not working! I am not at all happy about it!'

Technician: 'Okay, sir. What appears to be the problem?'

Customer: 'I've set everything up in accordance with the instruction manual but I can't go any further because for some reason the computer doesn't have a CD drive.'

Technician: 'No CD drive, you say? Well, it should certainly have one. It should be on the hard drive tower.'

Customer: 'Well, it isn't.'

Technician: 'Okay, sir. There should be a button on the drive tower that you press and then it slides open ready to accept your disk.'

Customer: 'There is a button but it's not working.'

Technician: 'In what way isn't it working, sir?'

Customer: 'Well, it's just not working. Don't you people understand plain English?'

Technician: 'What happens when you press the button, sir?'

Customer: 'Nothing much.'

Technician: 'What do you mean by "nothing much"?'

Customer: 'Exactly that: nothing much. There's no CD drive. The only thing that comes out is the cup holder.'

Technician: 'Thank you for calling technical support. My name is Carl. How can I help you?'

Customer: 'Where am I calling?'

Technician: 'Technical support. Are you having trouble with your internet connection, sir?'

Customer: 'I know that. I mean what part of the world?'

Technician: 'Oh, Canada.'

Customer: 'Canada?! You have the internet up in Canada?'

Technician (sarcastically): 'No, sir, we've just got radio really. In fact, I had to drive my dog sled into work. There was a horrible accident and I lost two dogs. It's been a rough day.'

Customer: 'Well, I want technical support from a country that actually has it!'

CLICK.

•

Customer: 'My keyboard isn't working.'

Technician: 'Is it plugged into the computer?'

Customer: 'I think so, but it's not easy for me to see behind the computer.'

Technician: 'Okay. Pick up your keyboard and walk ten paces back.'

Customer: 'Right.'
Technician: 'Did the keyboard come with you?'
Customer: 'Yes.'
Technician: 'That means the keyboard isn't plugged in.'
Customer: 'Oh.'

•

A woman rang a computer help desk to say that she couldn't switch on her new computer. After establishing that the computer was plugged in correctly, the technician asked her what happened when she pushed the power button. She said that she had kept pushing it but nothing ever happened. The conversation went on for several minutes as the technician tried to get to the root of her problem, until he suddenly realized the reason for her difficulties: the woman had been using the mouse as a foot pedal similar to the one she used to power her sewing machine.

•

Customer: 'I've got this problem. You people sent me this install disk, and now my A: drive won't work.'
Technician: 'Your A: drive won't work?'
Customer: 'That's what I said. You sent me a bad disk, it got stuck in my drive, and now it won't work at all.'

Techninican: 'Didn't it install properly? What kind of error messages did you get?'

Customer: 'I didn't get any error message. The disk got stuck in the drive and wouldn't come out. So I got these pliers and tried to get it out. That didn't work either.'

Technician: 'You did what, sir?'

Customer: 'I got these pliers and tried to get the disk out, but it wouldn't budge. I just ended up cracking the plastic stuff a bit.'

Technician: 'I don't understand, sir. Did you push the eject button?'

Customer: 'No. So then I got some butter and melted it and used a turkey baster and put the butter in the drive around the disk and that helped loosen it. Then I used the pliers and it came out fine. I can't believe that you would send me a disk that was broken and defective.'

Technician: 'Can I just clarify? You put melted butter in your A: drive and used pliers to pull the disk out?'

Customer: 'Yes.'

Technician: 'Did you push that little button that was sticking out when the disk was in the drive – you know, the thing called the disk eject button?'

Customer: 'Er, well, no, but you people are going

to fix my computer or I am going to sue you for breaking it!'

Technician: 'Let me get this straight. You are going to sue our company because you put the disk in the A: drive, didn't follow the instructions we sent you, didn't seek professional advice, didn't consult your user's manual on how to use your computer properly, but instead you poured butter into the drive and physically ripped the disk out?'

Customer: 'Well, I guess it doesn't sound too good when you put it like that.'

Technician: 'Do you really think you stand a chance, since we record every call?'

Customer: 'But you're supposed to help!'

Technician: 'I'm sorry, sir, but there's nothing we can do for you. Have a nice day!'

●

Customer: 'The screen is blue and it says Windows has been shut down because an error has been detected.'

Technician: 'Does it say press any key to continue?'

Customer: 'Yes.'

Technician: 'So do it.'

Customer: 'I've tried, but I've looked all over the keyboard and I can't find the any key.'

●

Customer: 'I received the software update you sent, but I still keep getting the same error message.'

Technician: 'Did you install the update?'

Customer: 'No. Oh, am I supposed to install it to get it to work?'

●

An elderly lady phoned a help desk and outlined the problems she was experiencing with connecting to the internet on her new computer. Running her through the standard troubleshooting procedure, he told her to place the cursor over the fourth icon from the left on the menu screen. 'Okay,' he said. 'It says Launch Internet Explorer Browser.' There was a moment's silence on the other end of the line before the old lady replied in wonderment: 'That's amazing! You can see my screen from there?!'

•

Customer: 'I need help setting up my internet connection.'

Technician: 'Okay, scroll down to the Windows button.'

Customer: 'Uh-huh.'

Technician: 'Then to the control panel.'

Customer: 'Uh-huh.'

Technician: 'Then networking.'

Customer: 'Did you want me to have the computer on?'

Technician: 'Yes!'

Customer: 'Okay, just a minute.'

•

A man called the help desk to say he was having problems with his computer. The technician went through a series of troubleshooting questions, at the end of which he said he was going to perform a short test on the computer. A few minutes later, he came back with the findings. 'Well, sir,' he said, 'I can't see any problem with this computer.'

The customer replied, 'Well, it's not *this* computer I have the problem with …'

•

Technician: 'I need you to right-click on the Open Desktop.'

Customer: 'Okay.'

Technician: 'Did you get a pop-up menu?'

Customer: 'No.'

Technician: 'Okay. Right-click again. Now do you see a pop-up menu?'

Customer: 'No.'

Technician: 'Okay. Can you tell me what you've done up to this point?'

Customer: 'Sure. You told me to write "click", so I wrote "click".'

•

Customer: 'I can't get on the internet.'

Technician: 'Are you sure you used the right password?'

Customer: 'Yes, I'm sure. I saw my colleague do it.'

Technician: 'Can you tell me what the password was?'

Customer: 'Five stars.'

•

Customer: 'Is the internet down?'

Technician: 'What, the entire internet? What makes you think that?'

Customer: 'Because I can't get onto it this afternoon on my computer.'

Technician: 'You probably just have a bad connection today.'

Customer: 'Oh, that's okay then. I didn't know if it might have been shut down by the government for some reason.'

Technician: 'I think that's unlikely, sir.'

Customer: 'Well, you hear about some of the terrible things on there – porn, Twitter trolls. I didn't know whether they'd decided to scrap it altogether.'

Technician: 'No, trust me, sir, the internet is still going.'

•

Customer: 'I can't print documents.'

Technician: 'Are you getting any messages on screen?'

Customer: 'Yes. It said the computer couldn't find the printer.'

Technician: 'So what did you do when you saw the message?'

Customer: 'I turned the monitor to face the printer, but it still said it couldn't find it!'

Customer: 'I recently bought a Compaq Presario SR1909UK but it didn't come with any software or cables. Could you send them to me?'

Technician: 'Which store did you buy it from?'

Customer: 'I didn't. I bought it from a guy in a pub.'

Technician: 'Sir, are you aware it could have been stolen?'

Customer: 'Well, I don't know! … I presume I do still have the full twelve months warranty on it?'

Technician: 'Can you open Windows for me?'

Customer: 'I'm afraid I can't.'

Technician: 'Why not, sir?'

Customer: 'I haven't got windows built in.'

Technician: 'You have Vista, sir. You must have Windows.'

Customer: 'I don't have windows or any kind of vista. I'm in a converted garage and I never built windows into it. If I open the door, will that help?'

•

While working on a computer help desk, Matt took a call from a woman who said she had a problem with her keyboard. She went on to describe how she had knocked a plant off her monitor and it had spilled dirt all over her keyboard. She wanted to know how best to clean it off. Matt told her that if soil had got right into the keyboard, it would be difficult to remove and would probably never work properly again. As keyboards are relatively cheap, he advised her to throw it out and pick up a new one at her nearest computer store. 'Throw it out?!' she cried indignantly. 'You must be joking! I paid hundreds of pounds for it!' Surprised by her reaction and thinking she must have some state-of-the-art model, he apologetically asked her what kind of keyboard she had. She replied, 'A Yamaha.'

ELECTRICAL GOODS STORE

Customer: 'Yesterday I came in here and bought a new lens for my camera but the lens cap is stuck on fast and won't come off. This is the second time I've had this problem. The one I bought before from another shop was also stuck and had to be replaced, so there must be some fault with the design. It's not good enough. You pay all this money for something and there's a basic flaw. It's shoddy workmanship.'

Assistant: 'Okay, let me take a look. How exactly have you been trying to remove the cap, sir?'

Customer: 'By twisting it, of course. I'm not stupid!'

Assistant: 'And which way have you been twisting it?'

Customer: 'Anti-clockwise – the same way as I always have. That's how they're supposed to twist off: anti-clockwise.'

Assistant: 'I know this is thinking radically outside the box, sir, but have you ever tried twisting it the other way?'

Customer: 'Don't be so ridiculous!'

Assistant: 'Just humour me, sir. Try it.'

Customer (fiddling successfully with the lens cap): 'Oh. (Pause) Well, it should be made clear on the instructions that this make of lens operates differently from every other model.'

A customer called a store to ask: 'If I load more songs on to my iPod, will it get heavier?'

•

Customer: 'I recently bought a dishwasher from you, but it's quite obviously faulty.'
Assistant: 'What makes you say that?'
Customer: 'Well, when I set it to wash, water sprays, but the plates don't spin.'

•

James was working in a city centre camera shop when a woman walked up to him and announced that the shop had completely ruined her daughter's fifth birthday party. When James asked what the problem was, the woman produced a camera from her bag that she said she had bought at the shop last month – specifically to take photos of the birthday celebrations – but to her extreme annoyance the camera didn't work. She was now demanding her money back. Before considering a refund, James asked if he could try the camera for himself. 'Be my guest!' she said sarcastically. 'But I'm telling you, it won't work. You've sold me a faulty camera.' James switched the camera on and everything seemed fine, but when he tried to take a picture the digital display indicated that there was insufficient memory. He then opened the battery compartment to inspect the memory card, only to find that there wasn't one. 'Where's the memory card?' he asked.

'Don't look at me!' she responded huffily. 'That's what I was sold in this shop.'

James explained to her that although she had the adapter, she also needed a memory card inside it. He asked her: 'Do you have something that looks like it would fit in this?'

'Oh, that little thing?' she scoffed. 'I threw that away!' Realizing from James's expression of disbelief that she had brought all her problems on herself, she quickly snatched up the camera and headed for the door, muttering darkly under her breath about a lack of clear instructions.

•

Customer (on phone): 'I bought some solar lights from you. Do you have anything to charge them with?'

•

Customer (on phone): 'I want to buy a TV. What's the cheapest one you have in stock?'

Assistant: 'Well, we have a thirteen-inch portable for £55.'

Customer: 'How big is that?'

Assistant: 'Er, thirteen inches.'

Customer: 'Yeah, but how big is thirteen inches?'

Assistant: 'A bit bigger than a foot.'

Customer: 'Yeah, but I have small feet. So I reckon I need something bigger. What's the next cheapest TV you have?'

Assistant: 'We have a fourteen-inch for £66.'

Customer: 'Is that bigger than the thirteen-inch?'

Assistant: 'Yes.'

Customer: 'How much bigger?'

Assistant: 'I'd say about an inch.'

Customer: 'Okay, I'll think about it.'

Assistant: 'You do that.'

●

Customer: 'Do you restore old photographs?'

Assistant: 'Yes, we do, madam.'

Customer: 'Excellent. Can you fix this photo for me?'

Assistant: 'Sure. What would you like us to do?'

Customer: 'Can you move the cow in the photo?'

Assistant: 'Move the cow?'

Customer: 'Yes, that's my great-grandfather sitting behind it, and I want to know what he looked like.'

Assistant: 'I don't think we can do that.'

Customer: 'Just move the cow over and we'll be able to see my great-grandfather's face.'

Assistant: 'I'm sorry. We don't have the technology to do that.'

Customer: 'Huh! Well, I suppose I'll just have to take this somewhere else.'

Customer: 'I bought a TV from you yesterday, but the remote doesn't work.'

Assistant (opening the back): 'That's because it doesn't have any batteries.'

Customer: 'Oh, does it take batteries?'

•

A woman went into an electrical store to buy a deluxe teasmade that boasted all the latest gadgets. The salesman patiently explained how it worked, telling her how to fill it properly and set the timer so that in the morning she would wake up to a nice freshly made cup of tea. A few weeks later, she returned to the store and the salesman, remembering her, asked her how she was getting on with the teasmade. 'Oh, it's wonderful,' she said. 'But there's one thing I don't understand. Why do I have to go to bed every time I want a cup of tea?'

PHONE AND COMMUNICATIONS SHOP

Customer: 'I'd like you to replace this mobile phone, please.'

Adviser: 'Why?'

Customer: 'Because this one's damaged and won't work.'

Adviser: 'How did it get damaged?'

Customer: 'It got wet.'

Adviser: 'How did it get wet?'

Customer: 'It was in the inside pocket of my jacket when I put it in the washing machine.'

Adviser: 'Why didn't you take the phone out first?'

Customer: 'I didn't think I needed to. The label on the jacket pocket clearly says "Fully waterproof".'

•

Adviser: 'So you get 1,000 minutes for $49.99.'

Customer: 'How many minutes?'

Adviser: '1,000.'

Customer: 'How much is this plan?'

Adviser: '$49.99.'

Customer: 'So I pay $50 for 1,000 minutes?'

Adviser: 'Yes.'

Customer: 'Really?'

Adviser: 'Yes.'

Customer: '1,000?'

Adviser: 'Yes.'

Customer: '50?'

Adviser: 'Yes.'

Customer: 'Hmmm … So how much would this cost me?'

•

David took a call from a customer who was complaining that he couldn't make outbound calls on his mobile phone. David asked the man whether he had the phone with him. 'Yes,' the man replied, 'I'm talking on it right now.' David did a mental double take to make sure he had heard the man correctly, and then said: 'So there can't be anything wrong with your phone. You just called me on it!' The embarrassed caller quickly hung up.

•

Customer: 'Are these prices in dollars?'
Adviser: 'Yes, they are in Canadian dollars.'
Customer: 'No, what is the price in dollars?'
Adviser: 'So you want to know what the price is in US currency?'
Customer: 'No, in dollars.'
Adviser: 'In US dollars?'
Customer: 'No! In dollars!'
Adviser: 'Are you from the USA?'
Customer: 'Yes.'
Adviser: 'Okay. Then I'll tell you the price in the dollars that you use in the US.'
Customer: 'Thank you.'

•

Customer: 'I get free mobile to mobile calling on my current plan, but I keep getting charged for mobile to mobile calls.'

Adviser: 'Okay. If you give me the numbers you are dialling, I can check them with the system … Thank you… Right … Now I see what the problem is. These numbers are with a different service provider and therefore do not qualify for mobile to mobile.'

Customer: 'But they're my neighbours'.'

Adviser: 'Yes, but your neighbours are not one of our customers.'

Customer: 'But they live in a mobile home!'

•

Customer: 'I bought a phone yesterday but it doesn't work.'

Adviser: 'Did you insert the batteries properly and charge it fully?'

Customer: 'What do I need to charge it for? It says wireless on the box! So shouldn't it work like a wireless? I should be able to switch it on and it should work straight away!'

•

Customer: 'I want a new phone. This one's broken.'

Adviser: 'So I see. What happened to it? It's in dozens of pieces.'

Customer: 'I ran over it with my truck – three times.'

Adviser: 'You ran over it in your truck three times? Deliberately?'

Customer: 'Sure. When you sold it to me, you said it was shockproof. Well it clearly isn't.'

Adviser: 'By shockproof I meant that if you were to accidentally drop it from a reasonable height, it wouldn't break. I didn't expect anyone to be so dumb as to deliberately run it over repeatedly in a truck.'

Customer: 'Well, you should have told me that at the start. But you didn't, so I want a new phone.'

Customer: 'I have a pager and I keep getting paged by somebody called Lucille. It amounts to sexual harassment, so I want you to stop her please.'

Adviser: 'Have you called her and asked her to stop paging you?'

Customer: 'She never leaves a number, so I can't call her back.'

Adviser: 'How do you know it's someone named Lucille if she never leaves a number?'

Customer: 'She leaves her name.'

Adviser: 'How does she spell her name?'

Customer: 'L-O-W-C-E-L-L.'

•

Customer: 'I want you to send a fax for me.'

Adviser: 'Certainly, madam. That's not a problem.'

Customer: 'But I want you to fold it in half before you fax it because it's confidential and I don't want just anyone being able to see it at the other end.'

•

Customer: 'My fax machine isn't working.'

Adviser: 'Can you give me a little more detail about the problem?'

Customer: 'Well, it's like this: I put the paper in that I want to fax but it's not going anywhere.'

Adviser: 'I'm sorry to hear that. What exactly do you mean when you say it's not going anywhere?'

Customer: 'Well, the paper keeps coming out of the other side of the machine and it's not going down the line.'

Adviser: 'I don't know how to break this to you, sir, but that's kind of how fax machines work.'

•

Customer (on phone): 'Can you give me the telephone number for Jack?'

Adviser: 'I'm sorry, sir, I don't understand what you're talking about.'

Customer: 'On page two, section seven of the user manual it clearly states that I need to unplug the fax machine from the AC wall socket and telephone Jack before cleaning. So can you give me the phone number for Jack as I can't find it anywhere in the manual.'

Adviser: 'Sir, I think you'll find it means the telephone point on the wall.'

•

COMPUTER SUPPORT 2

Customer: 'I can't get this software to install.'

Technician: 'Okay, what kind of CD drive do you have?'

Customer: 'I don't know.'

Technician: 'Well, what kind of computer do you have?'

Customer: 'I don't know.'

Technician: 'Do you know what version of Windows you are using?'

Customer: 'Yes, that I do know! AOL.'

•

Customer: 'I've lost my email. I can't see it anymore.'

Technician: 'Okay, madam. Can you open your browser for me?'

Customer: 'My what?'

Technician: 'Your browser. It's what you click on when you want to browse the internet.'

Customer: 'I don't use anything. I just turn on my computer and it's there.'

Clerk: 'Okay. Do you see the little blue "e" icon on your desktop?'

Customer: 'You mean I have to start writing letters again?'

Technician: 'I'm sorry?'

•

Customer: 'I don't have any pens at my desk. I just want my email again.'

Technician: 'No, madam. Your desktop, on your computer screen. Can you click on the little blue "e" on your computer screen for me?'

Customer: 'Oh, this is too much work. I'm too upset. Just send me my email. Can't you send me my email?'

Technician: 'Okay, madam, can you tell me what colour the lights are on your router right now?'

Customer: 'My what?'

Technician: 'The little box with a couple of green or possibly a red light on it. It will be near your computer.'

Customer: 'Lights and boxes, boxes and lights. Just get my email for me.'

Technician: 'My test is showing me that you should be able to get online. Can you tell me what you're seeing on your computer screen?'

Customer: 'It's been the same thing for the last two hours.'

Technician: 'An error message?'

Customer: 'No, just stars. It's black and moving stars.'

Technician: 'Do you see your mouse next to your keyboard?'

Customer: 'Yes.'

Technician: 'Move it for me.'

Customer: 'Move it?'
Technician: 'Yes, move it.'
Customer: 'My email!'

•

Customer: 'I have a problem. I've just been using my husband's keyboard for the first time but the enter key isn't working.'
Technician: 'How do you know?'
Customer: 'Well, whenever I hit the broken key, no information is accepted on screen. In fact, nothing happens except the cursor moves one column to the right.'
Technician: 'Okay. Let's try using the second enter key.'
Customer: 'What second enter key?'
Technician: 'Over on the right hand side of the keyboard is a number pad. There should be an enter key over there that you can use.'
Customer: 'Which one?'
Technician: 'It should say "Enter" or have a crooked arrow pointing to the left, depending on the keyboard model. It should look identical to the broken enter key.'
Customer: 'There's no key over there that looks the same.'

Technician: 'Well, what does the broken key say on it?'

Customer: 'It doesn't say anything.'

Technician: 'What does the broken key look like exactly?'

Customer: 'It's big and long, and doesn't have anything on it.'

Technician: '... And it's the one at the bottom of the keyboard?'

Customer: 'Yes, that's the one!'

Technician: 'And you say that every time you hit it, it just puts a space on the screen?'

Customer: 'Yes.'

Technician: 'That's because you're hitting the space bar!'

•

Technician: 'What's on your monitor now, madam?'

Customer: 'A teddy bear my boyfriend bought for me in the supermarket.'

•

Customer: 'My dad bought me a computer last week, and I was taking out a CD when the phone rang. I was also eating a pizza at the time, so I put the pizza on the open CD drawer so I could pick up the phone.'

Technician: 'What happened then?'

Customer: 'Well, the CD drawer took part of the pizza inside the computer. Now I can't get the drawer open. It's a real mess. Can you help me?'

Technician: 'This sounds very bad.'

Customer: 'I know! I need to get the pizza out because I'm really hungry.'

Customer: 'I can't log onto the internet.'

Technician: 'What error message are you getting?'

Customer: 'It's prompting me about wrong user ID/ password.'

Technician: 'Can I confirm that you are keying in your password in lower case?'

Customer: 'No.'

Technician: 'Your password needs to be in lower case.'

Customer: 'I can't.'

Technician: 'Why not?'

Customer: 'Because there are no lower case letters.'

Technician: 'Yes there are.'

Customer: 'This is bullsh*t! All the letters on the keyboard are in caps.'

Technician: 'Sir, I know this is difficult for you but just make sure the caps lock isn't on.'

Customer: 'Oh … okay.'

●

Technician: 'Thank you for calling. How may I help you?'

Customer: 'My computer don't work.'

Technician: 'I'm sorry to hear that, sir. Can I have the serial number off your CPU?'

Customer: 'My what?'

Technician: 'The computer tower.'

Customer: 'Huh?'

Technician: 'The tall thing next to your screen. Your hard drive.'

Customer: 'Listen, buddy, it's no use you trying to baffle me with technology.'

Technician: 'Okay, maybe I'm not expressing myself to you very well. Can you describe to me all the computer parts on your desk? I'll tell you which one has the number I need.'

Customer: 'It's just a keyboard and a screen, like any other computer.'

Technician: 'Oh, you have a laptop!'

Customer: 'A what?'

Technician: 'A computer you can take with you. The keyboard and screen fold together with a hinge in the middle. Right?'

Customer: 'No, wrong. I don't know what's up with you computer people today. First the sales guy tries to sell me a bunch of sh*t I don't need in this big box package and now you don't even know what a computer is! Brand new today and it don't even work!'

Technician: 'So … you just bought a keyboard and a monitor?'

Customer: 'What did I need all the rest of the sh*t in that box for? This was way cheaper. I ain't stupid!'

●

Customer: 'Can you please tell me how long it will be before you can help me? I've been waiting more than three hours.'

Technician: 'I'm sorry, I don't understand. What is your problem?'

Customer: 'I was working in Word and clicked the Help button over three hours ago. So I've been waiting all this time to hear from you.'

Technician: 'And now hit F8.'

Customer: 'It's not working.'

Technician: 'What did you do exactly?'

Customer: 'I hit the F-key eight times like you told me, but nothing's happening.'

•

Working in a computer call centre, Sean took a call from a customer who wanted to know what hours the centre was open. Sean told him that the number he had called was open twenty-four hours a day, seven days a week. Hearing this, the customer asked, 'Is that Eastern or Pacific time?'

•

Technician: 'Customer Support, how may I help you?'

Customer: 'I'm having trouble with Microsoft Word.'

Technician: 'What sort of trouble?'

Customer: 'Well, I was just typing along, and all of a sudden the words went away.'

Technician: 'Went away?'

Customer: 'They disappeared.'

Technician: 'Hmm. So what does your screen look like now?'

Customer: 'Nothing.'

Technician: 'Nothing?'

Customer: 'It's blank; it won't accept anything when I type.'

Technician: 'Are you still in Microsoft Word, or did you close it?'

Customer: 'How do I tell?'

Technician: 'Can you move the cursor around on the screen?'

Customer: 'There isn't any cursor. I told you: it won't accept anything I type.'

Technician: 'Does your monitor have a power indicator?'

Customer: 'What's a monitor?'

Technician: 'It's the thing with the screen on it that looks like a TV. Does it have a little light that tells you when it's on?'

Customer: 'I don't know.'

Technician: 'Well, then look on the back of the monitor and find where the power cord goes into it. Can you see that?'

Customer: 'Yes, I think so.'

Technician: 'Great. Follow the cord to the plug, and tell me if it's plugged into the wall.'

Customer: 'Yes, it is.'

Technician: 'When you were behind the monitor, did

you notice that there were two cables plugged into the back of it, not just one?'

Customer: 'No.'

Technician: 'Well, there are. I need you to look back there again and find the other cable.'

Customer: 'Uh, okay, here it is.'

Technician: 'Right. Follow it for me, and tell me if it's plugged securely into the back of your computer.'

Customer: 'I can't reach.'

Technician: 'Uh huh. Well, can you see if it is?'

Customer: 'No.'

Technician: 'Even if you maybe put your knee on something and lean way over?'

Customer: 'Oh, it's not because I don't have the right angle – it's because it's dark.'

Technician: 'Dark?'

Customer: 'Yes – the office light is off, and the only light I have is coming in from the window.'

Technician: 'Well, turn on the office light then.'

Customer: 'I can't.'

Technician: 'Oh? Why not?'

Customer: 'Because there's a power outage.'

Technician: 'A power outage, you say? Ah … okay, we've got it sorted now. Do you still have the boxes and manuals and packing stuff your computer came in?'

Customer: 'Well, yes, I keep them in the closet.'

Technician: 'Good. Go get them, and unplug your system and pack it up just like it was when you got it. Then take it back to the store you bought it from.'

Customer: 'Really? Is it that bad?'

Technician: 'Yes, I'm afraid it is.'

Customer: 'Well, all right then. What do I tell them?'

Technician: 'Tell them you're too stupid to own a computer.'

FOOD FAILS

BAKERY

A lady went into a baker's shop and bought a loaf of French bread for 99 cents. She wanted it cut in half, so the bakery did that for her, marking one half 99 cents and the other free. Seeing this, she complained that she was being charged 99 cents for half a loaf of bread. The next time she asked, the bakery marked one half 45 cents and the other 44. This time she complained that she was being charged twice.

•

Customer: 'Excuse me, could you decorate this cake for me?'
Baker: 'I'm sorry, madam, I'm just closing for the day. I'm afraid it will have to wait until tomorrow.'
Customer: 'You don't understand. I need it tonight for my daughter's sixth birthday party. I thought you stayed open until six o'clock.'
Baker: 'No, we always shut at four, madam.'

Customer: 'Well, it's not good enough. I got here as soon as I could after work. It's ridiculous closing so early. I shall call your manager!'

Baker: 'What do you do for a living, madam?'

Customer: 'I'm a dentist. Why?'

Baker: 'Would you be willing to look at my teeth after hours?'

Customer: 'That's different. My job is hard. Anyone could do your job.'

Baker: 'Then you won't mind taking that cake home and decorating it yourself.'

Customer: 'I ordered a pie for collection today.'

Baker: 'Can I have your name please?'

Customer: 'Mrs. Andrews.'

Baker: 'Ah yes, Mrs. Andrews: one strawberry pie.'

Customer: 'I know I ordered strawberry, but I've decided I want apple now.'

Baker: 'All our pies are made to order, so I'm afraid I can't change it.'

Customer: 'But I want apple now.'

Baker: 'But if you were to take an apple pie, someone who actually ordered apple will miss out. So you'll have to have the strawberry pie you ordered.'

Customer: 'But I don't want strawberry. You're asking me to pay for something I don't want.'

Baker: 'But you ordered strawberry two days ago. Not apple; strawberry.'

Customer: 'Well, if my dinner guests go down with food poisoning from eating strawberry pie, you'll be hearing from my solicitor!'

FAST FOOD OUTLET

Customer: 'What sandwiches do you have today?'

Retailer: 'Chicken, ham, beef, egg and cress, pork,

BLT, prawn, smoked salmon, tuna and cheese. But if you want cheese, I'm sorry; we're out of pickle.'

Customer: 'Out of pickle?! What kind of sandwich shop runs out of pickle?'

Retailer: 'I'm sorry, but for some reason we didn't get a delivery today. I was expecting one but I'm sure we'll have some pickle tomorrow.'

Customer: 'That's no good. I would have thought that pickle was an essential ingredient for any sandwich shop. The very least a customer would expect would be to have the option of pickle with a cheese sandwich. So to have none to offer is nothing less than a dereliction of duty.'

Retailer: 'I feel really bad about this now. Look, I'll tell you what I'll do: just for you I'll shut up shop for ten minutes and drive off to the supermarket and buy some pickle.'

Customer: 'No, don't bother; I don't like pickle.'

•

Al was working in a pizza parlour one evening when a caller complained that the half sausage, half pepperoni pizza that had just been delivered to his home was supposed to have the sausage on the left and the pepperoni on the right. Al politely suggested that the caller try turning the pizza around.

Customer: 'I'm confused about the buffalo wings.'
Server: 'In what way?'
Customer: 'I didn't know buffalo had wings.'
Server: 'They don't.'
Customer: 'So are these wings made out of buffalo?'
Server: 'No.'
Customer: 'Do they taste like buffalo?'
Server: 'No.'
Customer: 'I could have you up under the Trades Descriptions Act.'

A mother and her three-year-old daughter approached the counter of a fast food shop.
Customer: 'Tell the lady what you want, sweetie.'
Child: 'I want a hot dog.'
Customer (embarrassed): 'What do you say?'
Child: 'And make it fast!'

•

Customer: 'I ordered my burger with no tomato. But it looks like they put the tomato on and then took it off. There's three tomato seeds on there.'
Server: 'I apologize, ma'am. I'll get you a new one.'
Customer: 'I'm allergic to tomatoes, so do you know what would have happened if I'd eaten those three seeds?'
Server: 'Nothing would have happened to you.'
Customer: 'You obviously know nothing about allergies.'
Server: 'Maybe not, but I do know that if nothing happened to you after eating all the ketchup you put on your fries, nothing would have happened if you ate those three seeds.'

•

Server: 'And would you like a drink with your meal?'
Customer: 'Yeah, I'll have a cola.'
Server: 'Small or large?'
Customer: 'What's the difference?'

•

Customer: 'I want a large pizza with all the toppings.'
Server: 'All the toppings? We have seventeen different toppings. I'm not sure they'll taste that good together.'
Customer: 'But I'm really hungry – hungrier than I've ever been in my entire life.'
Server: 'Okay. So you want sliced banana on your pizza?'
Customer: 'Ugh! No way, not on a pizza. You can leave that off.'
Server: 'What about pineapple?'
Customer: 'No, I don't want fruit on a pizza. Leave that off, too.'
Server: 'Are you okay with anchovies?'
Customer: 'What are anchovies?'
Server: 'Little salty fish. We serve them in strips.'
Customer: 'No, I don't like the sound of them.'
Server: 'Tuna?'
Customer: 'No, forget the tuna. I'm not big on fish.'

Server: 'Olives?'

Customer: 'No, I hate olives.'

Server: 'Peanuts?'

Customer: 'No, I have a nut allergy.'

Server: 'In that case we'd better skip the almonds, too.'

Customer: 'Sure.'

Server: 'How are you on spinach?'

Customer: 'It's okay for Popeye, I guess, but I don't want vegetables on a pizza. It sounds too healthy.'

Server: 'So should I leave off the beetroot, too?'

Customer: 'Yeah.'

Server: 'And mushrooms?'

Customer: 'No, I definitely don't want mushrooms. They spoil a good pizza.'

Server: 'Pepperoni?'

Customer: 'Now you're talking! I love pepperoni. Mind you, it's eleven o'clock and I don't want anything too hot and spicy late at night. So perhaps on this occasion I'll skip the pepperoni.'

Server: 'Does that also apply to the spicy beef, chicken tikka, salami and extra garlic?'

Customer: 'Yeah, I guess so. Just to be on the safe side. I don't want to be up all night with indigestion.'

Server: 'Okay, so that's one ham and cheese pizza. It should be ready in fifteen minutes.'

Customer: 'Great.'

RESTAURANT

Customer: 'What's the soup of the day?'
Waiter: 'Pea and ham.'
Customer: 'Is that vegetarian?'
Waiter: 'Um, no … it's got ham in it.'
Customer: 'Can you pick it out? I don't eat meat.'

•

Some customers will try anything to obtain a free meal. A favourite scam is to put a few hairs in the food, blame a member of staff and refuse to pay. Experience had taught a young waitress, Elaine, to be on her guard, so when a man insisted that there was an unexplained hair in his lasagna she stood her ground. She told him the hair could only be from his head, but he stuck to his story and suggested that it must have come from the chef. So Elaine went into the kitchen and reappeared with the chef, still wearing his hat. The chef then removed his hat to reveal a shining bald pate. 'Now,' said the chef, addressing the customer, 'you were saying something about my hair being in your food?'

•

An American woman travelling in south-east Asia called at a restaurant where she was horrified to be served complimentary bird's nest soup. Refusing to taste a drop, she demanded to know if it was made from a real bird's nest. The waiter assured her that it was and explained that the bird built its nest using its own saliva as glue. The woman was disgusted, saying that there was no way she was going to eat bird's saliva. Realizing that there was no hope of converting her to this particular local delicacy, the waiter asked what she would prefer instead. 'Oh,' she replied, 'just fix me an omelette.'

Customer: 'What ice cream flavours do you have?'
Waitress: 'Let me see now; we have strawberry, raspberry, peach, pineapple, melon, orange, lemon, blackcurrant, passion fruit, coconut, dark chocolate, white chocolate, mint, chocolate and mint, coffee, caramel, kiwi fruit, banana and mango.'
Customer: 'No vanilla?'

Customer: 'These are the strangest mushy peas I've ever seen.'
Waiter: 'It's not mushy peas, sir. It's guacamole.'

Customer: 'I'll have the shrimp cocktail.'

Waiter (to second customer): 'Anything for you, or will you be sharing the shrimp cocktail with her?'

First customer (interrupts): 'Oh no, I am not sharing my shrimp cocktail with anyone! Tell me, what type of liquor is in it?'

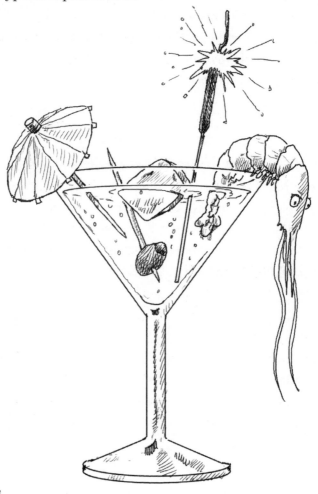

Customer: 'Can I order now please, waiter? I've got to be out of here in ten minutes.'

Waiter: 'Okay. What would you like, sir?'

Customer: 'A well done steak.'

•

Customer: 'I ordered this omelette, but I don't like it.'

Waiter: 'Is there something wrong with it?'

Customer: 'Yes. It smells like eggs.'

•

Customer: 'Pig's cheek? Tell me, waiter, what part of the pig is that from?'

HEALTH FOOD STORE

Customer: 'Excuse me, I can't find any bottles of Blank's vitamin pills.'

Assistant: 'I'm afraid we no longer stock them, madam.'

Customer: 'But I've bought them here before.'

Assistant: 'Recently?'

Customer: 'Fairly recently.'

Assistant: 'How recently?'

Customer: 'Uh … about eight years ago.'

Assistant: 'Well, I'm afraid we stopped stocking them because they weren't selling very well.'

Customer: 'But I liked them.'

Assistant: 'Yes, madam, but if you're the only customer buying them and you only buy them once every eight years, we'd soon be going out of business.'

Customer (stalking off): 'Typical! Everything's about money these days!'

•

Assistant: 'May I help you?'

Customer: 'Yes, do you have any pills that will make my wife look better?'

•

A woman approached an assistant at a health food store and asked, 'What flavour is this chocolate protein?'

•

Assistant (on phone): 'Good afternoon, Davison's Health Store. How can I help?'

Customer: 'I sent you a fax message five minutes ago. Did you get it?'

Assistant: 'I don't know. The fax machine is upstairs. What number did you fax it to?'

Customer: 'The same number that I'm calling right now.'

Assistant: 'Well, I'm afraid your fax message won't reach us. The number you're calling right now does not receive fax messages.'

Customer: 'How can you say that? I sent the fax and I got the beepy tone and the receipt and everything.'

Assistant: 'You had a fax message receipt confirmation?'

Customer: 'Sure I did. It's right here in front of me.'

Assistant: 'What does it say?'

Customer: 'Okay ... Let me see now ... It says ... "Fax Message Sending Failed."'

•

SUPERMARKET

A lady bought a single nectarine at the fruit department of a supermarket, but when the cashier scanned it, the customer complained that it was too expensive. 'I thought it was on offer,' she said. When the assistant explained that it was peaches that were on offer, not nectarines, the customer retorted, 'Well I'm not looking at it as a nectarine.'

•

Customer: 'What kind of sandwich is that?'

Assistant: 'Ham, madam.'

Customer: 'Just so long as it's not from a pig, that's okay.'

Assistant: 'No, madam, you don't understand: ham *is* from a pig.'

Customer: 'What are you talking about?! Chicken comes from a pig.'

Assistant: 'No, madam, I think you'll find chicken comes from a chicken.'

Customer: 'Well, it never used to. They keep giving these things fancy new names. How are people like me meant to keep up?'

•

Customer: 'I bought a large joint of beef from you last week and I would like a refund. It was terrible. In fact, it wouldn't surprise me if it wasn't beef at all, but horsemeat. It was full of gristle and totally inedible.'

Assistant: 'Could you possibly bring it in so that we can test it?'

Customer: 'Goodness, no. We've eaten it all.'

●

A woman walked into a supermarket and demanded a refund on a pack of mini bananas. She said she had bought them for her baby but her toddler had eaten them instead, so she wanted her money back.

●

Customer: 'Is this definitely beef, young man, and not horsemeat? Do I have your word for that?'

Assistant: 'Absolutely, madam. We sell only the finest quality meat. Take this joint, for instance: it won its last three races.'

Customer: 'That's not funny.'

●

Customer: 'Your organic pork. I need to know that the pig was free-roaming, not cooped up in a tiny pen.'

Assistant: 'Absolutely, madam. It had the run of the farm.'

Customer: 'And did it lead a happy life?'

Assistant: 'Idyllic, madam. It woke up every morning to panoramic views of the Lincolnshire Wolds. Even on the way to the abattoir I believe it was heard grunting how good life was.'

Customer: 'Very well. I'll have a pound and a half, please.'

•

A white woman, a black woman and a Mexican man were standing in the aisle of a supermarket. All three were wearing shirts with the company logo on front. A customer approached them and asked the white woman, 'Do you work here?'

'No,' she replied, sick of customers' stupid questions, 'we're triplets and our mother dresses us alike.'

•

Assistant: 'I'm sorry, madam, but the melon you have in your trolley is not for sale.'

Customer: 'What do you mean, it's not for sale?'

Assistant: 'It's for display purposes only.'

Customer: 'Well, then it should say so.'

Assistant: 'It does, madam. If you look, there's a large sticker on it saying "Not For Sale".'

Customer: 'Well, I was in a hurry. I didn't see it.'

Assistant: 'What I'll do, madam, is get a member of staff to fetch you another melon.'

Customer: 'I don't want to buy food that a total stranger has touched!'

Assistant: 'In that case, I suggest you go back to fetch a different melon.'

Customer: 'But I want this one.'

Assistant: 'I'm sorry, you can't have it. It's a display item. It's probably way past its sell-by date.'

Customer: 'It looks fine to me.'

Assistant: 'I can't sell it to you. It might not be safe to eat.'

Customer: 'Well, I haven't got time to go back. So we'll have to go without. (*Turning to her young son.*) The mean man won't let us have the melon.'

COFFEE SHOP

Customer: 'Could you make me that thing?'

Barista: 'I'm sorry?'

Customer: 'That thing. I was in here about six weeks ago and you made me something. Could you make it for me again? It was really good.'

Barista: 'That's a while back, ma'am, and we get a lot of customers. Tell me, this thing I made you: was it hot or cold, sweet or bitter?'

Customer: 'I can't remember, but it was really good. So could I just get one of those please?'

•

Customer: 'Is that a non-fat cappuccino? I asked for non-fat. Can you make sure it's non-fat? I want non-fat, okay?

Barista: 'There you go, madam: one non-fat cappuccino.'

Customer: 'Can you put some whipped cream on top for me?'

•

George was working in the coffee shop one afternoon when a woman approached the till with a bottled apple and mango juice drink. Rather than paying for it straightaway, as expected, she hesitated, asking, 'Is this vegetarian?'

•

Customer (on phone): 'Is my wife with you?'

Clerk: 'I don't know. It depends who you are. We have lots of wives in here at the moment. What does yours look like?'

Customer: 'Well, she's forty-five, although she could pass for fifty, she's short, overweight – to be honest she's let herself go a bit. A trip to the gym wouldn't do her any harm. Oh, and she's wearing a green cardigan that does absolutely nothing for her.'

Clerk: 'I think I can see her. What do you want me to tell her?'

Customer: 'Send her my love and say I'll be there in ten minutes.'

Sources

fuckyeahdumbcustomers.tumblr.com
notalwaysright.com
stupidcustomers.blogspot.com
www.callcentrehelper.com
www.phonephunnies.com
www.reddit.com
www.somethingawful.com
www.tenisionnot.com
www.theflyingpinto.com

Unexpected Item in the Bagging Area:
Driven crazy by the modern world?

ISBN: 978-1-84317-944-3 in hardback print format
ISBN: 978-1-84317-983-2 in ePub format
ISBN: 978-1-84317-984-9 in Mobipocket format

Are We Live?: The funniest bloopers from TV and radio
ISBN: 978-1-84317-866-8 in paperback print format
ISBN: 978-1-84317-963-4 in ePub format
ISBN: 978-1-84317-964-1 in Mobipocket format

Bad Teacher: Hilarious tales of staff misbehaving
ISBN: 978-1-78243-149-7 in paperback print format
ISBN: 978-1-78243-166-4 in ebook format